Ireland. Parliament House of Lords

The Debate in the Irish House of Peers

On a Motion Made by the Earl of Moira, Monday, February 19, 1798

Ireland. Parliament House of Lords

The Debate in the Irish House of Peers
On a Motion Made by the Earl of Moira, Monday, February 19, 1798

ISBN/EAN:

Printed in Europe, USA, Canada, Australia, Japan

Cover: Foto ©Suzi / pixelio.de

More available books at **www.hansebooks.com**

DEBATE

IN THE

IRISH HOUSE OF PEERS,

MONDAY, FEBRUARY 19, 1798.

THE

D E B A T E

IN THE

IRISH HOUSE OF PEERS,

ON A MOTION MADE BY THE

E A R L   O F   M O I R A,

MONDAY, FEBRUARY 19, 1798,

" That an humble Addrefs be prefented to his Excellency the Lord Lieute-
" nant to ftate, that as Parliament had confided to his Excellency extraordi-
" nary powers in order to fupport the Laws and defeat traiterous Combina-
" tions in this Country, we feel it our duty—as thofe powers have not pro-
" duced the defired effect—to recommend the adoption of fuch conciliatory
" meafures as may allay apprehenfions and difcontent."

FULLY AND ACCURATELY REPORTED.

D U B L I N :

PRINTED FOR JOHN MILLIKEN, NO. 32, GRAFTON-STREET.

1798.

IRISH HOUSE OF PEERS.

EARL MOIRA rofe. It is natural that I, who am not in the habit of frequently arrefting the attention of this Houfe, fhould be defirous of explaining the motives which have caufed me to appear before your Lordfhips. Contemplating the melancholy and the diftracted ftate of this country, I fhould feel myfelf loft to every fentiment of regard to my country, if I did not avail myfelf of my right to inftitute an inquiry into the caufes of this dreadful calamity. I am fcrupuloufly aware, my Lords, of the extreme fenfibility of the public mind ; I am aware of the danger of encreafing any anxiety or ill will which may exift in the country, and fhould be very far from appearing before your Lordfhips if I thought that any fpeech which I might make, or motion which I might offer, could be capable of irritating the feelings or exciting the paffions of the 'people of Ireland. There is one fubject which I feel it my duty to mention before I proceed to the

B   more

more immediate topic of my addrefs to your Lordfhips. I cannot pafs unnoticed the fcurrility which
the prints faid to be in the pay of Government have
ufed againft me. I lament that any Government
fhould have fallen fo low, fhould be fo fordid, fo illiberal, as to make the vehicles of public information the inftrument of detracting from perfonal exertion and the medium of moft foul and difgufting
fcurrility. As for my part, as far as it affects myfelf, I hold fuch means in contempt and deteftation,
and only regret that thofe who fhould fet the example of liberality and honourable demeanour, fhould
humble themfelves to fuch mean, paltry, and con-
temptible expedients; fuch calumnies I difregard,
and can only compare them to thofe mephitic va-
pours of the grotto del Cano, which, though they
are deftructive to animals who grovel, are by no
means dangerous or injurious to a man who walks
upright. It muft ftrike your Lordfhips, that I allude
to thofe charges which have been brought againft
me, when I defcribed in the parliament of the fifter
kingdom, the oppreffions which exifted in this country. Thefe repeated attacks have compelled me
to prefent myfelf before your Lordfhips, to ftate in
my place in this Houfe what I have already ftated
in the parliament of the fifter country, and to repeat them in ftronger terms, if poffible, than I there
afferted them. I ftated in the Houfe of Lords of
England, that, in many inftances, families had been
torn from their homes by their cruel and unmerciful
oppreffors,

oppreffors, without having any knowledge of the charge which was brought againft them, without being confronted with their accufers, without having the proofs exhibited to their view, and without any of thofe forms which the laws of the country had profcribed. This ftatement was made from proofs the moft ample and fatisfactory; fome facts had fallen within my own knowledge—of others I had received information from unqueftionable authority; indeed little is left for me to fay in fupport of that ftatement; a late decifion of the King's Bench had fhewn that fuch ftatement was not vain, idle, or il-lufory; I ftated that houfes had been burnt on loofe prefumptions of delinquency; I ftated too, that in fome inftances torture had been applied, and that picketing in many inftances had been reforted to, and that the unhappy victims of a mifguided fury were fometimes half hanged, or otherwife ill-treat-ed. Such a ftatement as this it was impoffible that I could have been induced to have made without clear and fatisfactory teftimony; it was a reprefentation too ftrong; it was, if untrue, an accufation too fe-rious to pafs unnoticed; at the bar of the Englifh Houfe of Lords I offered to fubftantiate this charge; I had the evidence prepared before I brought forward the accufation; before I made the ftatement I in-formed myfelf of the fituation of my country; fince my return I have further inveftigated the fubject, and I now re-affert, more pointedly, if poffible more ftrongly, that thefe cruel and fanguinary meafures have frequently been reforted to. There is another

topic,

topic, my Lords, which is a neceffary preliminary
to the immediate purport of my addrefs to you ; it
is another grofs, artful, and cruel mifreprefentation,—a mifreprefentation calculated to wound every
feeling of my foul, and exhibit me in a point of
view which my character has not, I hope, merited.;
poffibly, my Lords, this mifreprefentation may have
been occafioned by the ftrange incorrectnefs of the
London newfpapers ; I hope I may afcribe it to any
thing fo venial as incorrectnefs or mifconception.
To what I allude is my having been accufed of charging the army of Ireland with all the cruelties, all
the atrocities, all the barbarities which had taken
place in this country.   No, my Lords, never did I
prefume to charge the army with any acts of oppreffion ; the pride of my life is being a foldier, and
I love the character of a foldier too dearly to ftain it
by imputations of inhumanities ; from my earlieft
youth my pride was to be a foldier ; with every rank,
and with every department of the army have I been
converfant ; an attack therefore of fuch a nature
would lefs become me than any of my countrymen ;
and to the army, my Lords, it would be the more
galling, in as much as to receive a wound from a
FRIEND is more excruciating, more intolerable than
to receive it from any other perfon.   Surely, therefore, my Lords, it is natural that I fhould experience ftrong feelings of regret at this moft cruel and
to me the moft injurious miftatement.   No, my
Lords, comrades of every rank have always
been objects of my affection and folicitude,
                                                        and

and without vaunting of any perfonal exertions of my own, I think I have a right to claim the merit of being among the firft to reward loyalty and extend to my comrades in every rank, every comfort and every happinefs within my power. But, my Lords, exclufive of the perfonal love and veneration which I have for the brave defenders of my country, the very nature of the argument, and the very object I had in view, were fufficient to refute the calumny, and blunt the edge of this cruel and mifchievous mifreprefentation. What, my Lords, could have been more abfurd, what fo truly an object of aftonifhment, that at a time when I was arraigning the conduct of the Britifh Cabinet, when I was endeavouring to expofe its wicked and arbitrary fyftem towards Ireland, that I fhould change the ground of attack, and that I fhould act fo childifh a part as to exonerate the Cabinet, and throw the charge on my brother foldiers ? no, my Lords, it was againft the Cabinet of England that my attack was folely directed ; I accufed it of having made the army the inftrument of a cruel and arbitrary fyftem of vengeance and oppreffion towards this country. Under Heaven, I cannot conceive a more cruel and afflicting fituation for an officer, than a command in one of thofe proclaimed and perfecuted diftricts. When an officer is under the guidance of a magiftrate acquainted with the law, and called out to enforce it, his fituation is eafy, he is relieved from refponfibility ; but when he is vefted with a difcretionary power, his feelings are tremblingly
alive

alive to his military reputation; he ſhudders, left
his loyalty ſhould be queſtioned; high notions of
diſcipline ſtrongly ſeize on his mind, and regulate
his conduct; you touch, by placing him in this
ſituation, the worthieſt feelings of his heart; you
touch him on every principle which can animate
the boſom of a ſoldier; you touch him on his zeal,
his honour, and his courage. Sent into a part of a
country with which poſſibly he is unacquainted, his
difficulties are conſiderably augmented; he enter-
tains all the prejudices of education and early habits,
and from being told of the diſaffection which per-
vades the kingdom, he is, of courſe, inclined to
look with diſtruſt and ſuſpicion on the lower orders
of the community: impreſſed with the idea of
every man's plotting againſt the Government, timidity itſelf is conſtrued into diſaffection, and in the
dejected and broken looks of a wretched peaſantry,
he flatters himſelf with diſcovering the features of
revolt and inſurrection. Under this impreſſion it is
eaſy to account for numberleſs miſtakes and errors;
his countenance aſſumes the appearance of anger,
and his actions are marked with animoſity; it is
then that the ſeparation between him and the people,
which is commenced by the wicked arts of ſome
penſioned informers, is compleated, by mutual animoſity; to this the eſtrangement of affection of the
Iriſh officer from the Iriſh people alone is aſcribable;
thus it is that the wound which mildneſs and moderation might have cured and corrected, is fretted
and gangrened by thoſe foul and unworthy ma-
nœuvres.

nœuvres. With this view of the fubject, I am induced to call the attention of your Lordfhips to the fituation of your country ; and happy indeed fhall I be, fhould I be able to imprefs your Lordfhips with the neceffity of putting fome kind of termination to thofe moft cruel and diftreffing atrocities. The time, my Lords, is not yet loft for recovering the affections of your countrymen ; can you hope that you can reftore Ireland to peace by thefe acts of cruelty and oppreffion ? Conciliation may be deferred; but, every day that it is deferred, encreafes the difficulty of fuppreffing the views of the difcontented, and allaying the evils of infurrection and revolt. To difarm the republican, you muft concede to the loyalifts ; far be it from me by any ftatements which I may make, or argument I may ufe, to occafion ftill ftronger irritation. I conjure you to attempt comprize with the difcontented, and to abandon the conftant recourfe to military affiftance ; the interference of the army on thefe public occafions creates and inflames animofity ; it fufpends the wholefome and falutary influence of your laws, and exhibits you to the world as dependent for an exiftence, to military authority. To England this fyftem muft prove ruinous and deftructive ; involved in a conteft the moft obftinate and fevere, fhe requires every energy that this country could carry into the common caufe. Inftead of being threatened with becoming the feat of war herfelf, had fhe the cordial co-operation of this country, fhe may mock every effort which is made by her moft refolute and

implacable

implacable enemy : Bold in her declarations, does the French Republic afpire to ftake her exiftence with that of our empire itfelf, and difclaims every attempts which may be made for a pacific accommodation. If, my Lords, thefe perpetual plots, thefe conftant infurrections, can only be quelled by the bayonet, I am ftrongly apprehenfive, that inftead of the whole force of Great Britain and Ireland being directed againft France, the whole muft be directed to the fubjugation of this country. France, already formidable, great in military exertion, and having nearly accomplifhed all which in the commencement of the war fhe could have defigned, requires no civil diffenfions to make her prefent a frightful and terrific appearance ! Why does fhe not liften to peace ? Why difmifs your Negociator ? becaufe fhe fees the diftracted ftate of your country, and relies upon the diffentions which have been created here ; what then, fuppofing your fyftem to continue, muft be the fituation of the Britifh Empire ? how is fhe to be reprefented to pofterity, boldly ftruggling with a defperate antagonift ? No, fhe muft be exhibited at a time when the whole energy of the nation was requifite, when all was wanting ; torn by faction, broken down by diffention, a diminifhed power, and difmembered empire, at the utmoft reduced to an humble and injurious felf-defence, exclufive of this national degradation. Exclufive of the fhame, the confequence of this humiliation ; exclufive of the wound which the dignified feelings of this Houfe muft experience

for

for the country's being reduced to fo unworthy a
fituation ; what, fhould this dreadful fyftem continue, muft be the feelings, the individual feelings of
every man whom I now addrefs ; he returns to his
eftate, to contemplate in the circle of his tenants
and his neighbours, the heart-breaking difcontents which fuch a fyftem muft neceffarily occafion.
How can you bear, my Lords, to return to your
homes, to look on your tenantry with diffidence and
diftruft, to caft fufpicion on all you meet, and to
have thofe feelings rufhing on your mind that by
them you are confidered as their worft and moft implacable enemy ? Every caft of the eyes of your
peafantry in this fituation, you muft regard with
diftruft, and you have impofed on yourfelves the
hard neceffity of contemplating in the filent work-
ings of their hearts, the impreffion which they entertain of the injuries they experience from thofe
who fhould be the guardians of their comforts and
the protectors of their country. Need I expatiate
on the mifery which muft accompany fuch a fituation, and to men of liberal conception need I be ne-
ceffitated to point out the dangers and the evils
which accompany this ftate of diftruft, civil diffention and animofity ? This diftreffing fituation calls
to my recollection a beautiful apoftrophe which may
well be fuppofed in the mouth of a dejected country-
man.—" If an open enemy had been the author of
this, I could have borne with it ; if a ftranger, I
might poffibly have repelled it ; but fince thefe injuries have fallen from my old companion and friend,

C   1 know

not how to bear them." What perfon, my Lords,
acquainted with the infecurity of fuch a ftate, but
muft this night be inclined to co-operate in my humble attempt for its alteration.—" Nonne agitur mil-
" lies perire eft melius quam fua in civitate fine ar-
" matorum præfidio non poffe vivere? Aft ifthue,
" crede mihi, non eft præfidium. Caritate enim &
" benevolentia civium feptum effe oportet non ar-
" mis." The diffentions which thefe acts of outrage occafion, are not only deeply felt at home, but
they may render the fecurity of your country preca-
rious and uncertain; it makes you vulnerable to
your enemies, defpair operates moft powerfully on
the human heart; if you fhew no difpofition to al-
leviate the fufferings of the people, danger may become awful indeed. Let us be but united in fentiment, and to France and the world we may bid defiance; be but united, and it fignifies nothing if we
had not a fhip upon the fea; we may brave every attack; we would be certain of fruftrating any attempt of the enemy; do but abandon your fyftem
of feverity, your diftruft of the people, and thofe
horrid acts of outrage, and let France pour into either country her moft formidable levy, and I will
anfwer for it, my Lords, in one fortnight her army
will not appear, nay, will not exift in this country,
but in the CHARACTER OF PRISONERS; your fecurity is in your unanimity; the fums which you vote,
and the levies which you raife, are ufelefs, unlefs
you concede to the people; fecurity will then be
eafy to all. My Lords, let it not be faid, that con-
cession

ceffion would be ruin ; you undervalue the generous
character of your countrymen, they are not infenfi-
ble to kindnefs, they are alive to acts of friendfhip,
they can eftimate the value and importance of a benefit ; they will not, it is not in their nature to re-
quite friendfhip by ingratitude. In the heat of
party, and in the difturbed and agitated ftate of the
country, I fear that on both fides there have been
infinite mifapprehenfions ; you fay that plots have
exifted—that confpiracies have been detected—that
provocations have taken place in the country—
granted ; but have you not laws to reprefs this violence ? Are they not fufficiently forcible for this purpofe ? Do you complain of their wanting feverity ?
If you do, why not appeal to the wifdom of Parliament for fome, better calculated to fupprefs thofe
plots, to defeat thofe confpiracies, and to make the
people amenable to civil authority. If there are de-
linquencies, let the delinquents be punifhed, but
let them be punifhed by law ; deny not the common
rights of trial, tear not them from their homes, and
make them the victims of ungovernable fury. The
time to punifh was when men were proved to be
guilty, but forry am I that punifhment the moft fevere has been inflicted for offences the moft vague.
If fometimes exceffes did take place, vigour might
be ufed to reprefs them, but vigour is moft formidable when exercifed with moft prudence. All Governments are indebted for their fecurity to firmnefs,
juftice, and magnanimity, rather than to cruelty,
injuftice, and mifmanagement. I have abundance
of

of proofs to fhew you, that bare imputations of difaffection have warranted the moft arbitrary excefs of
power ; to be fufpected was enough to make the
poor peafantry of the country the fubjects of minif-
terial cruelty ; how dreadful that ftate of fociety,
when the liberty of the fubject is made dependant
on the whim and fufpicion of a low, illiterate, and
illiberal informer. So far, my Lords, I have been
general in my affertions, and general in my ftatement ; allow me now to ftate to you what has fallen
more immediately under my own obfervation. The
diftrict round my houfe, as I was affured, and, as
was generally underftood the year before laft, was
not merely difaffected, but tainted with rebellion ;
it was painted to me juft as far gone as any part of
the kingdom. When I returned there, it was natural that I fhould have the beft opportunity of tracing
thofe diffentions to their origin, and difcovering the
perfons who were fuppofed to be inftrumental in
organizing any plots, or forming any confpiracies,
exclufive of the poffibility of receiving information from my own peafantry—individual attachment gave me the beft grounds for thinking
that I had received the beft poffible information.
Finding that no fuch plots ever exifted, I ufed every
effort to difcover who were the authors of thefe calumnies, who it was who dared to proclaim this part
of the country in a ftate little fhort of infurrection
and rebellion. I did difcover, my Lords, the pre-
fumptuous wretch who paffed this foul calumny on
this part of your country. I traced it to an informer,

former, fo bafe, fo profligate, and fo abandoned, that there was not a Juftice of the Peace in that part of the country who could have believed him on his oath, if his intereft to the value of fix-pence was concerned ; and yet on the abandoned teftimony of this deteftable calumniator, the loyalty of the country was impeached, and the fevere interdict of difaffection, and its confequent penalties, pronounced upon the unfortunate people. Finding this to be the real truth of the tranfaction, I applied to have a declaration figned among my neighbours, expreffive of our attachment to the laws, our love of the Conftitution, and our determination to fupport both, as well as our Sovereign, with our lives and fortunes: I attended the meeting at which thofe refolutions were figned. Poffibly it may be faid, that thefe refolutions were mere words ; that the real fentiments of thofe who figned them were far different : to this I anfwer, it is not difficult to know when men are truly fincere ; there is a fimplicity and ingenuoufnefs about fincerity which never accompanies hypocrify and guilt, and if ever thofe features of fincerity ftruck a man as being characteriftic of the minds of the individuals, they ftruck me on that occafion : at that meeting I ftated to the people the nature of republicanifm, and likewife endeavoured to delineate the bleffings of a limited commonwealth, which, in fact, is the trueft monarchy. When I mentioned the ineftimable virtues of my Sovereign, there was not a man who did not exhibit the moft genuine and marked approbation. When I fpoke

of

of the magnanimity of his fon, the Prince of Wales, and the uniform attachment he profeffed for this kingdom ; when I mentioned the ftrong claims which the conduct of this country at the time of the regency had laid on the Prince's affection, and his confequent regard for our profperity and our peace. There was not an eye which did not beam gratitude, nor a heart which did not demonftrate its loyalty in the fervency of its acclamation. Since I have arrived in this country I have read the confeffions of Bird, alias Smith, Newell, &c. confeffions which were fufficient to wound every feeling of humanity, and ficken and difguft every feeling of the foul : thefe confeffions were demonftrative of the falfe and aggravated ftatements which Government was in the habit of receiving. I fhudder to think that fuch wretches could find employment or protection under any Government ; were not thefe things enough to urge Adminiftration to abandon its fyftem ; to enable them to contemplate the errors they had fallen into, and by an immediate relinquifhment of this intolerable feverity, to exhibit contrition at its having ever been introduced in this country ? Thefe were not times for crimination and recrimination, conceffions ought not to be regarded ; the generous confidence and manly warmth, the old nature of Ireland ought to be revived, and the years of difcomfiture and misfortune ought to be obliterated.

My Lords, the Government of Ireland is unacquainted with the true character of Irifhmen. I do declare moft folemnly, that I never knew the peafantry

fantry of any country fo fenfible of kindnefs, fo ea-
fily bound by friendfhip, with hearts fo grateful, as
the injured and infulted peafantry of this hard-fated
country. I know not that I can ftrengthen my
claim to your fympathy by any ftronger arguments
on this occafion—all that I have afferted in any other
Affembly I here re-affert, if poffible, in much
ftronger language. My intention is to " move for
" an Addrefs to the Lord Lieutenant, expreffive of
" our forrow at the fituation of the Country—how
" inadequate the meafures purfued have been to
" give peace and tranquillity to Ireland, and pray-
" ing that mild and conciliatory meafures may im-
" mediately be adopted." In this motion I have
fcrupuloufly avoided mentioning any inftances of
impropriety, and I have not alluded to any perfons
who may be fuppofed to be inftrumental in carrying
rigorous meafures improperly into execution; I
have left the motion open, and, as far as poffible,
unobjectionable. There are two fubjects, however,
of great magnitude, which, as being leading features of conceffion, I muft in this place mention;
the firft, as to the further extenfion of the privileges
of a people to the Catholics—on this fubject my
opinion was always decided—on it I never entertained a doubt. Under the prefent circumftances
of this country it was ungenerous and unjuft that a
great majority of the community fhould be ftamped,
with any mark or badge of fervitude, or compelled
to bear the galling reflections of being denied any
privileges enjoyed by their countrymen; fince this
country

country was declared free and independent, nothing could juftify one part of the community prefuming to enflave the greater portion of its inhabitants ; nothing could impede relaxation but a vicious, a jealous, and a proud monopoly. After what has been granted, little indeed remains to be conceded to the Catholics, what remains the Houfe fhould grant. His mind muft be ftrangely worked on who could argue for the expediency of thofe reftrictions which impeached the loyalty of a brave and magnanimous body of men, when an invading enemy threatened your fhores, and refted her fecurity on the diffentions which your rigorous penal code, and your proud monopoly of the rights of your countrymen had created. The fecond fubject, which was a fubject of the greateft importance, was the queftion of a parliamentary reform. The fentiments which he had expreffed in the Britifh Houfe of Parliament were fo much diftorted, mifreprefented and miftated, that he felt it the more neceffary to exprefs himfelf intelligibly and fatisfactorily on this topic. In that Houfe I did affert that I was not a friend to the fentiment of a parliamentary reform ; but though this was my opinion, yet it was an opinion which I entertained, not becaufe I faw parliamentary reform neceffarily occafioned thofe evils which fome think proper to afcribe to it ; my objection to parliamentary reform was on the ground of its not being practically expedient, and that I was apprehenfive that it might be attended with greater inconveniences in the experiment to carry it into execution, than advantages

vantages when carried into execution ; but this was always ftated as my private and humble opinion, unlefs the benefits which were to be the confe-quence of this meafure were more clearly defined ; I have, it is true, objected to that meafure; but whate-ver might have been my doubts as to the advantages of Reform of England, my doubts are certainly not fo great with refpect to this country ; I have ever confidered the queftion as completely Confti-tutional, and ever muft I reprobate that fyftem which treats with intolerance men who are admirers of this improvement. My doubts with refpect to the propriety of Reform in Ireland, are greatly re-moved, when I fee and know, that the public mind in this country is bent on that meafure, when I know that a fentiment in its favour has feized the whole community, I venture not to queftion its ex-pediency ; the people of Ireland feel they are unre-prefented ; the Parliament of Ireland has declared Reform a falutary expedient, it would be indecent to doubt or queftion its utility, when this is the cafe, *I think Reform ought to be conceded.* I am free to declare that the mifchief which may be occa-fioned by not conceding it, may be much greater than any mifchiefs which might follow the con-ceffion. I beg, therefore, to be underftood as the friend to Reform in Ireland ; becaufe Reform is confidered by the people as a great meafure for re-ftoring the peace, and fecuring the happinefs of the country ; on this motion there are many points for argument, two great meafures of this nature

D   would

would footh the mind, and fufpend the apprehenfions of the people; Parliament is now called upon
to make fome declaration; this is not a common
occafion, the common duties of humanity fhould
urge the Houfe to an adoption of this much-wanted
meafure, a declaration of the opinion of the Houfe
to the Lord Lieutenant would warm the fentiments
of all claffes, would revive affection; the ftate of
the country ought minutely to be weighed; if it
is unpleafant to grant, it fhould be remembered
that it may be dangerous to withhold; conceffion may be offered too late; the time is not yet
paffed, and the hiftory of mankind and of the world
fhews the danger of abandoning any favourable
opportunity which may offer for the accomplifhment of any great object of national utility. His
Lordfhip concluded his fpeech with the following
motion :

" That an Addrefs be prefented to his Excellency
" the Lord Lieutenant, reprefenting that as Par-
" liament hath confided to his Excellency extra-
" ordinary powers for fupporting the laws and
" for defeating any traiterous combinations
" which may exift in this kingdom, this Houfe
" feels it, at the fame time, a duty to recommend
" the adoption of fuch conciliatory meafures
" as may allay the apprehenfions and extin-
" guifh the difcontents unhappily prevalent in
" this country."

LORD

LORD GLENTWORTH. My Lords, It is not my intention to excufe myfelf for thus early offering my fentiments, by making any parade of affected modefty. The tendency of the motion made by the noble Lord, is in my mind, fo mifchievous, that it fhould be met as early as poffible. Much depends, my Lords, upon the turn which this debate fhall take ; upon it depends, whether the loyal and well affected fpirit of the nation fhall be invigorated by your decifion of this night, or whether a feditious faction fhall be animated by an apparent encouragement of their treafons ; whether order fhall be up-held in this country, or rebellion be fuffered to put down thofe who have fupported the laws and civilization of Ireland.

I beg to affure the noble Earl that whatever I fhall fay cannot be intended unkindly towards him ; for him perfonally I feel the higheft refpect ; I have not indeed the honour of being acquainted with him, but I read the hiftory of the times which have lately paffed by, and I find there his worth and his merits record-ed; but it is my duty to canvafs any public meafure however brought forward, it is a duty which I owe to your Lordfhips and myfelf; and a duty from which I will not fhrink. My Lords, this is a fub-ject not altogether new to your Lordfhips; it has been already treated in the Britifh Parliament. The noble Earl fpeaks of the pride of Irifh independence ; I have the honour to be a member of the Irifh Legi-flature, and I muft fay that to bring a fubject, treating the interior concerns of this kingdom before another

another Parliament, was, to give it no harsher name, an infringement upon that independence. I have seen in the newspapers, perhaps incorrectly, the grounds upon which that measure was justified ; it has of late been a custom in the desperate plunges of a British party, to bring forward Ireland in all debates for their own party-purposes ; and indeed, my Lords, I am the less astonished at this attack of that party upon our independence, when I consider the conduct of one of their leaders towards this country upon a very important occasion.

In the year 1782, when Mr. Eden (now my Lord ukland) brought forward in the British House the repeal of a statute, which, as it no longer disgraces the English code, I may venture to call an infamous statute—the 6th of Geo. I. The distinguished leader of this very party (Mr. Fox) then a servant of the Crown, stated that he never had heard of a measure so daring ; that it was a measure which went to lay Great Britain at the feet of Ireland ;—that act was repealed, that blasted act, which deprived your Lordships of your appellant jurisdiction upon a pretence that you had abused it, which left you, indeed, coronets and robes, but deprived you of any influence or respect in the country. To this opinion that party leader still adheres, and he is in consequence always ready to trifle with the independence of Ireland to suit his own purposes.

The noble Lari has, however, more affection, more regard, and more feeling for the independence of the country, in which he has large possessions,

splendid

fplendid honours, and great refpect; and he has not acted thus without attempting to juftify his con-duct. That juftification he has made upon the grounds of precedent and neceffity; the Britifh Parliament was fitting; the Irifh was not; the danger was imminent, and the time preffing.

If his expreffions have been rightly ftated, the noble Earl wifhed to be examined upon oath as to the facts he alledged in the Britifh Houfe; I know the accuracy of the noble Earl, and I know that he muft have wifhed to be examined as to facts within own knowledge; that he would not fo folemnly venture to retail the ftories of agitating phyficians and factious tradefmen; of the emiffaries of treafon, or traitors; the noble Earl muft therefore have been in this country at the time of thofe outrages which he has deplored; and if he were in Ireland, why did he not come to his Majefty's Chief Governor, as his duty directed him, and call upon him to put a ftop to the evil? I have not heard that he did fo; if the danger was imminent, was not here an imme-diate refource? If the time was preffing, was not here the obvious and fpeedy remedy without delay? But the meafure has been juftified by precedent—by that of the Duke of Lauderdale. Suppofing, my Lords, for a moment, that the precedent did apply; are we to go back to the times antecedent to the Revolution for precedents to act upon at this day? If we were to do fo, there is not an act of outrage, cruelty, or oppreffion, which might not be fuftained by a pre-cedent. But I will take the liberty to fay that the

cafe

cafe of Lord Lauderdale does not apply; the English Parliament took cognizance of his conduct, becaufe he was a member of the Englifh Cabinet of that day. Is Lord Camden fo? I believe not; and I am confident in the pofition, that no man or body of men ought to have, or have, a right to controul or judge his conduct, but the Parliament of Ireland, and the King of Ireland wearing the crown of Great Britain, to which that of Ireland is infeperably, and I truft for ever, united.

My Lords, I cannot exprefs my opinion of this conduct in any other way than fuppofing the mover to have faid to the people of Ireland, " Your own " Parliament is too corrupt and too infufficient, it " is unequal to the entertainment of fuch a dif- " cuffion, I will therefore bring forward your inde- " pendent interefts to be difcuffed by the Britifh " Parliament.".

Governments are of human inftitution and liable to error, it is not furprifing therefore that we hear of abufes in Adminiftration; I have heard, my Lords, of other countries and other parliaments where men have been introduced into the Commons Houfe, with whom no other member of that Houfe would in any other place have difgraced himfelf by holding converfation; I have heard, (I do not fpeak of this Parliament,) I have heard that in other Parliaments men of mean conduct, low manners, and low birth, have been introduced amongft your Lordfhips to fit in this Houfe, to hide their polluted heads under the coronet of nobility.

I fpeak

I fpeak my Lords, of other days, and other Parliaments. But, my Lords, look to the conduct of our
Parliament for the laft fifteen years ; fee what has
been its unvaried labour; has it not given to this
country within that time the bleffings of the Britifh
Conftitution ? Is this a difpofition of hoftility to the
people ? Is this a conduct deferving of flight or in-
attention ? The noble Earl feems to complain, that
the unfortunate ftate of the country has arifen from
fevere and coercive meafures, adopted by Government ; with great deference I beg leave to obferve,
that he miftakes the effect for the caufe. The noble
Earl difapproves of the meafures of the Britifh Cabinet, and of the Irifh Government ; I do by no
means defend all their meafures—I difapprove of
many—but the times are too wild, the crifis too
momentous, for any man to play the paltry game of
vanity or emolument : I agree that Adminiftration
has not been blamelefs, but it is becaufe they did
not begin fooner that I blame them ; that they did
not at firft act with more vigour, and then we fhould
not be reduced to the deplorable fituation in which
the country ftands.

The noble Earl wifhes to draw a veil over the
enormities which have difgraced this country. To
juftify my conduct to the world, and to myfelf, I
wifh to withdraw that veil and fhew to the noble
Earl a concealed fcene of horrors with which he
feems utterly unacquainted. Firft, my Lords, allow me to obferve, that the prefent war which is held
out as the fource of all our evils, had proceeded for
a confiderable

a confiderable time previous to the operation of a moft diabolical confpiracy againft the peace and happinefs of this country; that this country felt no part of its calamities; that they were beheld at a diftance, as a tragic reprefentation, in which we fuffered in nothing but in our feelings of humanity and pity; that our manufactures and our trade were increafing; that our linen exports had amounted to a fum never known before; that the exports of the South had increafed; that our agriculture flourifhed beyond the fondeft fpeculations, and, that the whole country appeared to profper even amidft the afflictions of Europe; until men were found like the Devil in Milton, to ficken at this fcene of happinefs, and, as they could not enjoy, to determine to blaft it. The noble Earl is too well informed how lamentably they have fucceeded; he fees the effects, though he has completely miftaken the caufe. In accomplifhment of their malignity they have by two talifmanic expreflions torn the bofom of the country; by Parliamentary Reform, aud Catholic Emancipation.

As to Catholic Emancipation, it is not now the time for me to debate it; many of the Catholic body are loyal in fpite of all the efforts to feduce them; many others who have been feduced, are now convinced of their errors, and anxious to return to their duty. They are told that they are flaves, becaufe fome of the great Offices of State are not in their power; becaufe the office of Chancellor is not within their reach, and, becaufe their

Gentry

Gentry cannot fit in the other Houfe of Parliament: the Proteftants are told that they are flaves, becaufe they have not a Parliamentary Reform ; becaufe a vifionary undefined project is not made the law of the land. It is too true of human nature, that the mind of man is never fo fitted to receive perverfe opinions, as when he is moft happy ; our ifland was happy when thefe opinions were firft promulgated, the peafant at his plough was told of the cruelty of order, and the injuftice of an inequality of ranks ; he was told, " while you labour others fleep ;" it was a doctrine too palatable to man, not to be received with avidity ; fo far the purpofe of its authors fucceeded ; they then went farther—they faid this evil could not be removed while we were connected with another country in which thofe ranks exifted, and a country in which happily thofe doctrines have made little progrefs.

In the month of June 1795, treafon was fo mature in this country, that a perfon was fent from the difaffected of Ireland, to treat with the Government of France ; that perfon remained for fome time at Paris, and, having been fufficiently inftructed, returned to purfue the good work of organizing infurrection in this country. Do your Lordfhips forget the very curious paper which was proved before your Committee to have been written by the founder of the Society of United Irifhmen, upon its firft eftablifhment ? You cannot—it is extant in the records of Parliament, and in the mind of every man who remembers the hiftory of this country ; but

F.   your

your Lordſhips may have overlooked the very extraordinary coincidence which it bears to the plans of
the Geman *Illuminati*, ſo lately diſcovered by the
learned Profeſſor Robiſon; if your Lordſhips will
look into thoſe plans, you will find them recommending the very ſyſtem purſued by the United
Iriſhmen ;—have your Lordſhips ſeen the proſpectus
of the United Iriſhmen, upon which their founder
ſo much improved ? If you have not, I hold it in
my hand, and as there is one paſſage peculiarly applicable to the debate of this night, and clearly prov-
ing the uſe which is intended to be made of any countenance which the diſaffected may derive from the
conſtructive ſupport of thoſe who may appear to favour them, I cannot avoid reading it to your Lordſhips.

" *When the ariſtocracy come forward, the people fall
backward : when the people come forward, the ariſtocracy, fearful of being left behind, inſinuate themſelves
into our ranks, and riſe into timid leaders or treacherous auxiliaries—they mean to make us their inſtruments. Let us rather make them our inſtruments.
One of the two muſt happen—the people muſt ſerve the
purpoſes of party, or the party muſt merge in the
mightineſs of the people, and then Hercules will lean
upon his club.*"

This, my Lords, is the key-ſtone, the grand ſe-
cret of the United Iriſhmen : this is ſufficient warn-
ing to any man of prudence, who regards his honour, his life, or his property. All theſe are attacked by this abominable ſyſtem ; all theſe are to
be defended by timely vigour.

This

This envoy returned my Lords in the month of June 1796; your Lordſhips will recollect with what activity the work then went on. You will recollect the robberies, the murders, the midnight meetings which diſgraced that time; that when any of theſe men fell under puniſhment of the law, jurors were attacked, were told that if they preſumed to find according to their oath, they ſhould not only be marked themſelves, but that if they ſhould return to their habitations, they ſhould find no houſes to cover them, no families to receive them.

Then rebellion ſtalked boldly abroad, encouraging its friends and affrighting its enemies. . What was the language of the diſaffected? " Look at thoſe we " wiſh to puniſh; does any one of them eſcape? " Look at thoſe who offered againſt the laws; are " any of them puniſhed? Government cannot pro- " tect you; we can. The Great Nation is coming " to our aid, join with us, and we will ſhare our " advantages with you; ſupport the Government " and periſh along with it."

The French did come—their fleets were diſperſed by the winds of Heaven—they were ſcattered over the waves of the ocean. One would have hoped my Lords, that treaſon would have ſunk in deſpair; on the contrary, this very failure was uſed as a new argument and a new ſtimulus to treaſon. It was ſaid, " ſee, the boaſted ſuperiority of the Britiſh " navy is not ſufficient to protect your ſhores from " invaſion; accident has prevented our wiſhes once; " it may not a ſecond time." And my Lords, ſo

convinced

convinced were they of a fecond attempt at invafion, that a meeting was held in May 1797 in the county of Down, at which even perfons of fome property were prefent—when it was debated ferioufly, and nearly agreed to, that a rifing and maffacre fhould take place immediately.

This came to the ears of Government, and it was thought neceffary to come forward ; this was done by directing the gallant General who commands in the northern diftrict, to call in all the arms which were within his command.

This act of Government was laid before Parliament—the opinion of Parliament was called for ; that opinion was given approving of the meafure ; and yet it has been faid that thefe people were only miftaken, and that they thought they had a right to retain the arms thus demanded.

It was the imperious neceffity of the time which brought Government thus forward ; had it not fo come forward it would have deferted its duty : We have heard of fhocking inftances of feverity my Lords; I lament that feverity fhould have become neceffary ; I lament that where the arms were found of which the weak or the loyal had been plundered, that fuch feverity was neceffary for the fake of example : But I am by no means inclined to fuppofe that any unneceffary feverity was authorifed by the orders of Government ; if I thought Government had fanctioned an act of outrage, I fhould not be its advocate.

The

The orders given to the military were : That as the magiſtrates of the country had been intimidated from acting, the military ſhould act as magiſtrates. In the execution of thoſe orders it is poſſible that outrages may have happened ; but thoſe outrages were far from having any ſanction or authority from Government.

Government has been accuſed of fomenting diſſenſions between religious parties in the northern counties, and affording a ſort of countenance to one of them. I know of my own knowledge, that a letter was written from Government to a noble Viſcount who ſits near me, directing him to hold an even hand between all parties ; to repreſs violence by whomſoever committed, and to act with undeviating juſtice towards all deſcriptions. And here my Lords allow me to obſerve, that much has been ſaid in reprobation of ORANGE-MEN as oppoſed to DEFENDERS or UNITED IRISHMEN. I do not at all approve of combinations ; but I muſt ſay that the DEFENDERS are avowedly aſſociated for the overthrow of the Conſtitution, the ORANGE-MEN for its maintenance. If combinations are at all to be approved, I cannot heſitate in ſaying which beſt deſerves approbation.

My Lords, I know that I addreſs the firſt aſſembly of the land : I will not ſtate therefore any thing which I have not the beſt ground for believing to be true. At the moment when your negociator was at Liſle, there was alſo there a negociator from the traitors of this country, and there is good reaſon

fon to think that the Irifh ambaffador had much
more frequent intercourfe with the French minifter
than my Lord Malmfbury had ; that he urged the
French to make no peace with Great Britain; that his
arguments were of this kind : " Her trade is em-
" barraffed, her credit fhaken, her people divided.
" In Ireland you have friends ; what avail a few
" petty iflands which if you can attack her in Ire-
" land fhe muft reftore ?—*Carthage muft be deftroyed.*
" —Land in Ireland and ftrike her to the heart.
" If what you have demanded already, be acceded
" to, make the firft part of your *projct* the inde-
" pendence of Ireland on Great Britain. By this
" will be meant feparation ; I know that England
" not accede to it ; but by doing this you will
" encourage your friends in Ireland." And my
Lords, I do moft certainly believe that if our ambaffador had acceded to the full powers demanded
by the French, thefe very terms would have been
amongft the firft propofed.

Another fact, my Lords, is well authenticated,
that at this very moment an accredited envoy from
the traitors of Ireland, is received by the Directory
of France—is now refident in Paris, and paid by
the traitors of this country ; and that he has ga-
thered round him every difaffected out-caft of the
empire, from the cowardly demagogue Napper
Tandy to Mr. Muir, from the coaft of South America ; that within a very fhort time paft, a project
of invafion has been forwarded to France, in which
our traitors exprefs their readinefs to rife ; mention

tion the places proper for landing—ſtate that they have men and money enough, but want arms ; and defiring the French to bring but a ſmall body of troops.

The noble Earl has talked of newſpapers in the pay of Government ; I know of none ſuch, but every man muſt know that there are ſome in the ſervice of treaſon, vilifying every authority and diſturbing every diſtrict of the country.

I know à newſpaper in this city which many of your Lordſhips have ſeen, which labours continually to advance the ſyſtem of treaſon ; and I find much fault with Government for not putting down that paper with a ſtrong hand ; the ſtrong hand of the law ; for I cannot ſuppoſe that the laws can be deficient, when ſuch an outrage againſt ſociety is publiſhed.

Another paper I hold in my hand, my Lords, it is the *Union Star* ; and I own I cannot expreſs my ſurpriſe at a report of a ſpeech of the noble Earl in another country ; a report, which I hope, was inaccurate ; in which he is ſaid to have charged this paper as a fabrication of Government to excuſe its own enormities ; I will, my Lords, read a few words from this very horrible publication, to prove how juſtly that charge has been made ;—after ſtating the names and deſcriptions of the perſons who are recommended to public vengeance ; it goes on thus :—

" *We certainly do not adviſe, though we do not de-*
" *cry aſſaſſination ; as we conſider it to be the only*
" *means*

" *means in the power of the people of Ireland, to avenge*
" *themfelves upon the royal agents, who carry death,*
" *and terror, and deftruction through this devoted*
" *country.*"

" *Oh ! fhade of the venerable Brutus, who didft*
" *ftab the tyrant of thy country in the midft of his cor-*
" *rupt and venal Senate, &c.*" here your Lordfhips
will obferve a good deal of French phrafeology ;—
Brutus is the hero of the French Republicans, and
his example is offered as the model for Irifh traitors.

This paper, my Lords, is circulated throughout
the country, it is forced upon the people ; it is
put into their hands as they pafs the ftreets, and
thrown into their Houfes ;—with fuch arguments
urged upon the lower orders, who can be furprifed
at affaffination ?

In the other Paper, my Lords, which I have
fpoken of (the PRESS) * the hope of a French invafion has been always held forth as the hope of
this country ; and laft Saturday, (in what contem-
plation the thing was written I know not)
the mafk is completely thrown off, and the people
of Ireland are thus addreffed ; Your Lordfhip's
know that it is the nature of man when he goes
unpunifhed for one crime to commit greater ; and
to advance with encouraged audacity, as he finds encreafed impunity. Would France endure this their
boafted France—would not the authors of fuch treafon againft the government of France have long
fince paffed over the Atlantic ocean into exile
or under the guillotine into eternity.

I fuppofe

* Prefs, Feb. 17th, 1798.—See Appendix.

I fuppofe, my Lords, from what I have faid, their malignity may be directed at me ; but I truft that my mind is fuperior to their attacks, and that in the difcharge of what I feel my duty, I can defpife the malice of Treafon.

I fhall totally pafs over the caufes of difcontent and confufion which the noble Earl is faid to have ftated in another country, the failure of our trade and the decay of our manufactures. I truft that, the noble Earl, fince his arrival in this country, has had better information ; for I obferve that he has not reafferted thofe caufes in this Houfe. It is moft certain, my Lords, that in this city there was much diftrefs ; but it was the effect and not the caufe of the difturbances which have difgraced the country ; the terror of the times had affrighted many of the rich from the confumption of thofe manufactnres which had employed fo many hands heretofore ; that diftrefs does not exift now ; the linen manufacture is now nearly as flourifhing as ever, and as to the provifion trade of the South, it is in more profperity than ever was yet known.

I am happy that the noble Earl has not thought it neceffary to cite particular inftances of accufation againft the government of this country ; I am happy becaufe it proves that he is by no means concerned with fome perfons not the moft loyal, who had juft before his arrival formed themfelves into a fociety for the collection of grievances. I fhould have been forry to fuppofe him capable of taking his information from fo polluted a fource.

F   In

In the report which has been circulated of the noble Earls fpeech, he is faid have fpoke of the *corfeu* as eftablifhed in this country—your Lordfhips well know how hateful the *corfeu* is in England—and coupling the enormities of the United Irifhmen, with the oppreffion of the *corfeu*, was in England fome fort of juftification of them; what is this *corfeu*?—a law that in a difturbed diftrict, proclaimed upon a memorial to Government, the labourers and manufacturers fhall be reftrained from running about the country, to commit robbery and affaffination; in other parts of the country not proclaimed, no fuch regulation does exift.

The half hanging the unfortunate peafantry is an accufation to be found in this fpeech, it is worth your Lordfhips while to hear, upon what this charge is founded, I have myfelf acquired into the fact and can ftate it with truth. An officer of the Wicklow militia was ordered out at night to prevent an intended outrage on the houfe of a farmer in the county of Kildare; he had not got far when he heard regular platoon firing, he haftened to the fpot and found the infurgents attacking the farmers houfe the farmer* was defending himfelf with great refolution, and not knowing whether the new comers were friends or enemies, he continued his defence, and one foldier of the militia was unfortunately killed from the houfe; two of the infurgents who were taken in the very fact of affaulting the houfe, fell

* Mr. Sparks of Carbery.

fell upon their knees and implored mercy; they offered
to tell all they knew and to give very material information, the officer with equal prudence and
humanity, fpared their lives, but when they were
brought to his quarters they abfolutely refufed to
give any account whatfoever ; a rope was put round
the neck of one of them, and the officer threatened
to hang him over his fhoulder, nothing further was
done, and yet this is one of their enormities of
which the Irifh Government has been accufed, and
I have no doubt that moft of the others have the
fame fort of foundation.

My Lords the midnight hour would furprife us
if I were to enter into a detail of the horrors committed by treafon in this country ; I fhall juft
mention to the noble Earl a few of their affaffinations,
in the county with which he is acquainted, and
almoft immediately clofe to his own refidence.
(Here his Lordfhip read a long lift of perfons
murdered in the county of Down in 1796 and 1797,
amongft the reft the names of James Stevenfon,
Abraham Edwards, Daniel Morgan, John Comyn,
Jofeph Harper, &c. &c.)

In the month of November laft, a foldier of the
Limerick militia was induced when drunk, to take
the oath of treafon to his fovereign and allegiance
to France; he informed againft his feducers, they
were taken, and he was for fafety ordered to be cautious in his conduct, his fteps were however watched
by the friends of the accufed, and when he was found
to be too cautious, a woman was made ufe of as
their inftrument, the wife of one of the accufed, fhe

went

went to the foldier, told him fhe had long loved him, fhewed him a purfe of money and entreated him to fly with her; the wretched man was enticed to accompany her, and, about half a mile from his quarters, while her arms were folded round him in apparent fondnefs, the hatchet of an accomplice clove his head in twain. Are your Lordfhips acquainted that a court is eftablifhed even in the city of Cork by thefe traitors, for the trial not only of thofe who are of the body, but of all other perfons ; that to thofe whom they fufpect, a certain fet of interrogatories are put, their hands tied behind them, and their brains blown out by order, and in the prefence of that court.

It is not two months, my Lords, fince at Two-mile-bridge, near Youghal, a poor man, his wife, his child, and his maid fervant, were all murdered by thofe traitors, and, horrible to think, one of the murderers was the brother of the maid fervant, who dared not refufe ftabbing his own fifter, at the com-mand of his diabolical rulers.

I hold in my hand, my Lords, a melancholy pa-per : it contains a recital of the murder of an excel-lent and gallant officer; an officer who had long ferved with honour and reputation in his Majefty's armies. This worthy man had gone to his eftate, in the county of Cork, to influence his tenantry into quiet : the kindnefs of his heart, and the generofi-ty of his manners, were well adapted to that pur-pofe. Hear, my Lords, from the depofition of the unhappy Mrs. Uniacke, the miferable event of his honourable defign.

[Lord

[Lord Glentworth here read the depofition of Mrs. Uniacke, widow of the late Jafper Uniacke, Efq. of Ariglyn, county of Cork, ftating, that on the 9th of February, 1798, Manfergh St. George, Efq. had dined at the houfe of Ariglyn, that while Mr. St. George was going to his bed, and Mr. Uniacke attending him with a light, a number of perfons entered the houfe, and leaving others on the outfide, rufhed into the room in which the deponent fat with her infant child, and paffed on to that in which Mr. St. George and her late hufband were; that fhe ran with her child up ftairs, and was ftopped by the ruffians who were affailing her hufband; that fhe was beat to the ground, and while fhe lay there, the body of Colonel St. George was drawn over her ; that fhe heard a blow given to her hufband, which founded hollow upon his fkull, and that he never groaned afterwards, &c. ! ! !]

And, my Lords, even upon this barbarous murder, which would difgrace the cannibals of America, has The Press made a comment, which only in Ireland could have paffed unpunifhed—" That if the people be urged into outrage, it is only wonderful that enormities are not more frequent." I have read, I think, a fentence like this made ufe of by an advocate, who took advantage of his fituation at the bar, to utter a libel on the Conftitution.

Since I came into the houfe this evening, I have been informed by an officer of high rank, that two privates of the ninth dragoons were murdered, on the night before laft, with circumftances of the moft horrid barbarity ; that one of them was abfolutely

lutely hewed into pieces, and the other left hanging on a tree, near the mangled remains of his fellow foldier; thus, by the arts of treafon, are fo many Irifhmen transferred into a band of affaffins. We have read with horror of the affaffins of Syria; of the Old Man of the Mountain: here are affaffins more active, and directors more concealed; wretches who fit behind the fcenes, and order the affaffinations which they have not fpirit to attempt. My Lords, if I can conceive Government at all unjuftifiable, it is in not having acted fooner: I am happy to fee that they at laft do act, and I hope that activity will continue.

The noble Earl fpeaks of conciliation; with whom are we to conciliate? Is it with traitors leagued with France? Will you, my Lords, concede your properties, your families and your lives? With nothing elfe will they be fatisfied; and are you prepared to make fuch a conceffion? The conceffions of Reform and Emancipation would be to apply a petty plaifter to a gangrened wound. Let me entreat the noble Earl to confider the danger refulting from a man like him ever feeming to countenance the projects of difaffection. He has feen in America the horrors of civil war; he knows that the danger in civil war is not over when the parties have left the field; he knows that acts are committed on both fides, which, however juftifiable, call for mutual retaliation; he knows, that a gallant General now commanding in this country had nearly fallen a facrifice to that unhappy neceffity, and furely he will not aid in reviving it in Ireland. I appeal to the fame magnanimity,

ty, which has fo often led him to diftinguifh his gal-
lantry in the field, to exhibit a ftill greater exercife
of that magnanimity : I entreat him, if he feels, as
he muft feel, that this country has been greatly mifreprefented, that he will prove that magnanimity
by owning that he has been in error, and by with-
drawing his motion. My Lords, I have to apolo-
gize for fo long detaining you : I fhall not longer
do fo, than to fay, that if rebellion be not inftantly put down, rebellion will put you down.

The EARL of CAVAN rejoiced that the noble
Earl had difavowed the expreffions in which he
was reported to have fpoken fo haftily of the military character. It became that noble Earl to
do fo ; and as he had done fo, he thought the
noble Earl fhould go farther, and profecute the
printer of a pamphlet publifhed in this city within thefe two days, and purporting to be his fpeech
in which this attack on the military was fet forth
in the moft unequivocal terms, a nobleman who
revered the military character fo highly could
hardly refufe them this juftice. It had been
faid of the foldiery that they had obeyed orders
as foldiers, at which their feelings as men re-
volted ; this he felt a fevere imputation on
himfelf and the other General Officers of Ulfter,
who muft have firft received thofe orders from
Government, and he trufted that every man who
knew them had too high an opinion of their feelings
to fuppofe that they, would obey orders inhuman cr
tyrannical, if Government could have iffued them ;
but he muft fay, that to his certain knowledge,

no

no orders had ever iſſued which could bear ſuch a conſtruction. His Lordſhip ſaid, that the zeal, ſteadineſs and loyalty of the troops in the quarter where he had the honour to command, weɪe beyond his praiſe, whenever their exertions were neceſſary, they were prompt, and thoſe exertions were often neceſſary; men had aſſociated themſelves together under a name which ought to include every thing honourable and patriotic, the name of United Iriſhmen.; yet was there a man in the kingdom who did not know that they were aſſociated for traiterous purpoſes! If there was any circumſtance which could give him more pride than any other, it was that by his Seat in that Houſe he was enabled at this time to declare his firm attachment to his Sovereign and the Conſtitution; an attachment, from which neither the attacks of rebels, nor their anonymous menaces ſhould ever ſhake him. Aſſaſſination had been the lot of many who had dared to manifeſt this attachment; it might be his:—it was a fate againſt which no man could guard; it was a fate to which every man obnoxious to treaſon was now liable; but this apprehenſion had no weight with his mind: his ſentiments were too much fixed to be altered by it. He would conclude by one obſervation: The noble Earl had ſtated enormities to have exiſted; why did not the noble Earl apply to the next general officer to have them redreſſed, when he heard of them, inſtead of carrying the recital of them without explanation into England, and detailing them in the Britiſh Houſe of Peers?

LORD

LORD CHANCELLOR.—I am happy to have an opportunity of difcuffing this fubject with the noble Lord in this affembly; I know of none on which there has been fuch a feries of ftudied and perfevering mifreprefentation, and certainly very liberal contributions have been made to the Common ftock, under the fanction and authority of the noble Earl's name. If we are to believe reports apparently well authenticated, which have been nearly avowed this night on his part, the noble Earl has twice brought forward this fubject in the Britifh Houfe of Lords. His firft propofition to that grave affembly was, to addrefs his Majefty to interpofe his gracious and paternal interference to allay the difcontents fubfifting in the kingdom of Ireland, which threatened the deareft interefts of the Britifh empire. One principal fource of Irifh difcontent he ftated to be, that the Irifh Catholics infifted on their right of fitting in both Houfes of Parliament, from which they are precluded by the ftatute law of Ireland. Another caufe of offence to the people, the noble Lord ftated to be, that a Member of the Irifh Houfe of Commons had, uninvited and without any apparent neceffity, ftarted up in a debate and pronounced an abfolute interdiction on the hopes and pretentions of Irifh Catholics. That another member in the other Houfe of Parliament had equally uninvited and without neceffity, ftarted up in *his* place, and pronounced a fweeping condemnation

G   on

on the North of Ireland. I will not take upon
me to fay what might have paffed in the Houfe
of Commons, but I do, with perfect confidence,
affure the noble Lord, that nothing has paffed in
this Houfe fince I have had the honour of fitting
in it, which can give a fhade of juftice to an imputation thus caft on one of its Members. The
noble Earl, if we are to credit written and verbal
reports, for the authenticity of which I can in fome
fort vouch, has recently again brought forward
the fame fubject in the fame affembly, when without making a diftinct propofition upon it, *he* certainly did in the accepation of plain underftandings
pronounce a fweeping condemnation upon every
department of the ftate, civil and military, in the
kingdom of Ireland ; when *he* did in the accepta-
tion of plain underftandings reprefent the executive
government as acting wantonly on a fyftem of infult and barbarity againft an innocent and unoffending people, and the army of Ireland as active
inftruments in carrying it into rigorous and unrelent-
ing execution. And let me here with the unfeigned
refpect which I feel for the name and character
of a liberal and high minded gentleman, and a
gallant foldier, put it to the noble Lord's good
fenfe on cool and mature reflection, upon what
principle he could feel himfelf juftified in paffing
by this Houfe of Parliament, of which he is a
Member, and making an appeal to the Britifh
Houfe of Lords, on a fubject folely and exclufively

fively cognizable by the Parliament of Ireland ;
let me put it to his good fenfe, upon what principle he could feel himfelf juftified in preffing
the Britifh Houfe of Lords to addrefs his Majefty, to interpofe the influence of the Crown
to allay difcontents in Ireland, which he ftated
to arife from the operation and effect of Irifh ftatutes, an addrefs of the Britifh Houfe of Lords to
his Majefty to interpofe the influence of the Crown
to procure a repeal of Irifh ftatutes, of deep and
momentous import to the conftitution of Ireland.
Let me put it to his good fenfe, if he has not
been traduced, upon what principle he can juftify
a rafh an ill-advifed affertion, that a member of
this Houfe had, uninvited and without neceffity
ftarted up in his place, and pronounced a fweeping
condemnation on the north of Ireland, and having
made the affertion, urge it as a ground for an addrefs
of the Britifh Houfe of Lords to his Majefty, to
interpofe his authority againft the effects of this
affumed Parliamentary indifcretion in a peer of Ireland, or perhaps to prevent a repetition of it. And
above all, upon what principle he could feel himfelf
juftified in a ftatement to the Britifh Houfe of Lords ?
that the executive Government of Ireland had
taught the foldiery to confider and to treat the natives of this country indifcriminately as rebels, and
under fuch a fuppofition, to goad them with wan-
ton and unexampled infult and barbarity. That
the obfolete feudal badge of fervitude, the curfew,

was

was now revived and eftablifhed in all its rigour in Ireland, and enforced by the foldiery with unfeeling cruelty and infult. That the infamous and deteftable principles and proceedings of the inquifition, had been introduced into Ireland, where the unhappy natives were put to the torture, to extort from them a confeffion of their own guilt or the guilt of others; where the unhappy natives were torn from their families and immured in prifons, ignorant of their accufers, and in a cruel ftate of uncertainty as to the period of their imprifonment, and the fate which awaited them. And that thefe complicated and unexampled exceffes and extravagancies formed only a part of the fyftem acted upon by the executive Government of Ireland, and encouraged by the Britifh Cabinet. And thefe virulent and diftorted exaggerations have paffed into general circulation through the medium of every difaffected and feditious public print in Great Britain and Ireland, under the proffered folemnity of the noble Lords' oath. It remains for me publickly and diftinctly to refute the foul and injurious charges of tyranny, injuftice and oppreffion upon the people of Ireland which have been advanced againft the Britifh Cabinet and the Britifh Nation, and againft the Government and Parliament of Ireland ; and in fo doing, I fhall give the beft anfwer to every thing which has fallen from the noble Lord this night.—It has long been the fafhion of this country to drown the voice of truth and juftice by noife and clamour and loud and confident

fident affertions ; and fince the feparation of America from the Britifh empire, where the noble Lord well knows fome Britifh politicians had fuccefsfully played a game of embarraffment againft Lord North's adminiftration, they have been pleafed to turn their attention to Ireland, as a theatre of political warfare, and to lend their beft countenance and fupport to every motley faction, which has reared its head in this country, to difturb the publick peace for the moft felfifh and mifchievous purpofes. When the noble Lord recommends conciliation as a remedy for the turbulent and diftracted ftate of this country, with ali refpect for him, I muft conclude, that his information flows from this polluted fource. If conciliation be a pledge of national tranquillity and contentment ; if it be a fpell to allay popular ferment, there is not a nation in Europe in which it has had fo fair a trial as in the kindom of Ireland. For a period nearly of twenty years, a liberal and unvaried fyftem of conceffion and conciliation has been purfued and acted upon by the Britifh Government. Conceffion and conciliation have produced only a frefh ftock of grievances, and the difcontents of Ireland have kept peace with her profperity ; for I am bold to fay, there is not a nation on the habitable globe, which has advanced in cultivation and commerce, in agriculture and in manufactures, with the fame rapidity, in the fame period. Her progrefs is now retarded, and it is a heart-breaking fpectacle to every man who loves the country, to fee it arrefted

only

only by the perverfe and factious folly of the people, ftimulated and encouraged by difappointed ftatef-men, Britifh as well as Irifh. When the noble Lord talks of conciliation as the certain means of tran-quillizing the country, I call upon him to fay what fecurity he can give us for the accomplifhment of his prefage. Does he fpeak from experience? Evident-ly not; experience is againft him. When Lord North opened the trade of the Britifh colonies and plantations to Ireland, Parliament declared itfelf fully gratified in terms of warm and affectionate fa-tisfaction; and be it remembered that fome of the loudeft modern declaimers in the Britifh Parliament for Irifh emancipation, did then oppofe this firft re-laxation in the fyftem of commercial reftrictions, impofed by Britifh ftatutes upon Ireland, at the Re-volution. In a few months however the voice of indignation and complaint was again heard in the Irifh Houfe of Commons, and although the en-croachments on our conftitution and its defects which were then complained of, were generally ad-mitted to exift, a confiderable majority in both Houfes of Parliament thought it unwife and impo-litic to bring them forward in terms of anger and apparent hoftility to Great Britain, more efpecially at a time when fhe laboured under the preffure of an extenfive and calamitous war. An appeal was then for the firft time preferred from the decifion of Par-liament to the armed Majefty of the People, and without any form or folemnity of trial, or delibera-tion, every gentleman of Ireland who hefitated to

declare

declare open war againft the Parliament of Great
Britain, was denounced as an enemy to his country,
by that candid and auguft tribunal. However, on
a change of adminiftration in 1782, the Britifh Government determined to accede to the demands of
Ireland, and adopted a proceeding which, of all
others, feemed to be the moft flattering and conciliatory to the Parliament and People. The Duke of
Portland, by the King's command, fent down a meffage to both Houfes of Parliament, " That his Majefty was concerned to find that difcontents and jea-
loufies prevailed amongft his loving fubjects of Ireland on matters of great weight and importance, and
recommending that the fame might be taken into fe-
rious confideration, in order to fuch final adjuftment
as might give mutual fatisfaction to Great Britain
and Ireland." If ever there was a proceeding devifed, which might afford a rational hope of quieting
the apprehenfions and relieving the exigencies of a
diftreffed country, it was this appeal to their own
teftimony, for a knowledge of their complaints, to
defire them to come forward and to ftate the meafure
of their calamities, and the beft expedient for the
relief of them. And accordingly the meafure of
conceffion and conciliation, demanded of Great
Britain, for the final adjuftment of all political
controverfy between the two kingdoms, and for
their mutual and lafting fatisfaction, was framed on
the declared fenfe of the Irifh Oppofition-Cabinet ;
for on looking into the Journals it will be found,
that the addreffes in anfwer to his Majefty's moft

gracious

gracious and conciliatory meffage, were moved and voted by way of amendment, propofed by the leaders of the popular caufe in both Houfes of Parliament. And the noblemen and gentlemen who undertook the office of pointing out the grievances of Ireland, for a redrefs which was to lead to a final adjuftment of all political divifions between this kingdom and Great Britain, confined them, " To the ufurped claim of the Britifh Parliament to make laws for Ireland : to the appellant jurifdiction exercifed by the Britifh Houfe of Lords : to the practice of fuppreffing Bills in the Council of Ireland, or of altering them any where, and to a Perpetual Mutiny Law." In the progrefs of the fame Seffion, a communication was made to both Houfes of Parliament, in a fpeech from the Throne by the Duke of Portland, " that the Britifh Parliament had paid immediate attention to our reprefentation, and that his Majefty would gracioufly give his Royal Affent to fuch Bills as might be neceffary to give them full effect." To this communication, an anfwer was made by an Addrefs of both Houfes of Parliament to his Majefty, and to the Duke of Portland. This Addrefs was alfo framed by the Cabinet of Oppofition. The noblemen and gentlemen who had originally taken upon them the office of pointing out the conftitutional grievances of Ireland, were the movers of it, and did with peculiar eloquence exprefs the acknowledgments of the Parliament and People of Ireland, for the prompt and dignified attention which

which had been paid to their reprefentations. In the Addrefs moved by them, and adopted by both Houfes, they affured his Majefty, that " We were fully fenfible of the magnanimity of his Majefty, and of the wifdom of his Parliament of Great Britain, in feconding his Majefty's moft gracious intentions to this kingdom, without any ftipulation or condition whatfoever, *and that his Majefty might have the firmeft reliance upon the faith, generofity and honour of the Irifh nation. That as it is their un- doubted intereft, fo it is their warmeft wifh, to promote and perpetuate the harmony, ftability and glory of the Britifh empire ; and that the fame fpirit which induced them to affert their right to fhare the freedom of Great Britain, will confirm them in a determination to fhare her fate alfo, ftanding and falling with the Britifh nation."* The Commons went a ftep beyond this Houfe : they affured his Majefty, " *that from thence- forward no conftitutional queftion could by poffibility arife to interrupt the harmony fo happily eftablifhed be- between Great Britain and Ireland,*" and voted the enormous fum of fifty thoufand pounds, out of the public purfe, as a gratuity to the Gentleman who had thus pledged himfelf and pledged Parliament to a final fettlement of conftitutional grievances be- tween the two countries, a fettlement fo complete and fatisfactory, as to render a revival of political or conftitutional controverfies utterly impoffible. This Addrefs was echoed with unbounded applaufe from end to end of the kingdom, and the founders of the new Irifh Conftitution, were, for the fhort period of

H   a few

a few weeks, the idols of the People. Unfortunately, in that fhort interval, all harmony was at an end. A Gentleman of diftinguifhed ability difcovered, that the fimple repeal of a declaratory law, did not contain a renunciation of the principle which had been declared ;. from whence he argued, that our new Conftitution was a bubble, that the Irifh nation had been duped by the Britifh Minifter and Parliament, and that the noblemen and gentlemen who had undertaken Irifh emancipation (it was at this period I think the phrafe got into ufe) acquiefcing in the deception, muft be confidered as accomplices in the treachery of Great Britain. To this abftract propofition, and to the inference drawn from it, immediate and general affent was given, and a gentleman who had been raifed to the pinnacle of popular favour and applaufe, for acknowledged public fervices, inftantly became the fubject of popular execration, and was loaded with foul and moft unmerited calumny and abufe, for no other reafon than his refufal to concur in committing the Parliament of this country in a quarrel with the Britifh nation, upon this abftract rule of interpretation which was affumed to apply to all declaratory ftatutes, and to eftablifh unequivocally the infincerity of Great Britain. It is not neceffary now to examine the merits of the abftract legal queftion, but this I do not fcruple to fay, that nine hundred and ninety-nine men in one thoufand, who fo loudly condemned the act of Simple Repeal, were utterly incapable of forming an opinion on the fubject ; and

that

that if from the fame authority they had been told,
that an act of Renunciation was an infult to the nation, inafmuch as it implied an exifting principle to
be renounced, the men who fo loudly condemned a
fimple repeal, would have been equally noify againft
renunciation. But I fhould have hoped that this
grofs and glaring inftance of popular levity would
have taught the fober part of the community, and
more efpecially the gentlemen who had well nigh
fallen victims to it, the imminent hazard of inflam-
ing the popular mind upon abftract political topics,
and of making appeals to the majefty of the people,
for the redrefs of fpeculative political grievances.
At the fame period the majefty of the people was a
fecond time affronted. We had in the warmth of
our gratitude, and before the fimple repeal bubble
had been difcovered, voted away almoft every regiment of infantry on the Irifh eftablifhment, for the
fervice of the Empire, infomuch that there were
not foldiers left in the country for common garrifon
duty. The Duke of Portland, with no other poffible view than to provide for the neceffary fervice of
the kingdom, on terms the moft œconomical, raifed
four provincial regiments to be difbanded at the conclufion of the war. This was conftrued to be an
infidious fcheme of the Britifh Government, to un-
dermine the popular inftitution of Volunteers. If
fo many regiments of the line had been raifed, and
the eftablifhment had been incumbered with half-pay
for the officers, I prefume the majefty of the people
would not have been offended ; but a fencible regiment

ment was new in Ireland, and without further enquiry or confideration, this neceffary act of public
duty, adopted by the Duke of Portland upon a mere
principle of public œconomy, was generally and
loudly condemned as a frefh inftance of Britifh
infincerity. It happened foon after the Duke of
Porthand had quitted the Government of this
kingdom, that the Judges of the Court of King's
Bench at Weftminfter, gave their judgment upon a record removed by writ of error brought
there, from the King's Bench of Ireland; and no
man who knows the law will fay, that they could
have done otherwife. They found a record removed
into their Court by authority of the King's writ,
and finding it there, they could not avoid giving
judgment upon it. This however raifed a new ferment in Ireland, and this judicial act of Lord Mans-
field and his brethren, was reprefented here as a
direct violation of Britifh faith, and an open and
unequivocal attack upon the Irifh conftitution.
Lord Buckingham was then Lord Lieutenant of Ireland, and although I was not then a fervant of the
Crown, having lived in early habits of friendfhip
and intimacy with him, I can from my knowledge
ftate, that with a firm conviction that Great Britain
had always intended, fully, fairly, and unequivocally to renounce all legiflative and judicial authority over this country, he felt the warmeft anxiety
to fatisfy the people of Ireland that their fufpicions
were unfounded; that whether the act by which the
Britifh Parliament yielded their legiflative claims,

was

was an act of fimple repeal, or an act of renunciation, they might and ought to place full and firm
confidence in the faith and honour of Great Britain
as their beft fecurity ; but it was ftated to him that
there were Britifh ftatutes unrepealed made for the
protection of trade, particularly to the Eaft Indies,
by which penalties were inflicted upon Irifh fubjects
for breach of them committed in this country, and
that fuits for the recovery of thefe penalties were,
by the fame ftatutes, cognizable in the King's fuperior Courts at Weftminfter ; and it was ftated to him
that the mere repeal of the declaratory act of the
6th Geo. I. would not be fufficient to bar any fuit
which might be fo inftituted, but that an-act of renunciation would be conftrued by the Englifh judges
as a virtual repeal of all laws heretofore made which
imported to bind Ireland. Lord Buckingham therefore plainly faw that fuch an act was neceffary for
the peace of both countries, and warmly recommended to the Britifh Government to have it propofed in Parliament. Accordingly a Bill was introduced into the Britifh Houfe of Commons I believe
by his brother, now Lord Grenville, which paffed
into a law without oppofition, renouncing in terms
the moft unequivocal all legiflative or judicial authority in Ireland, declaring the right of the people of
Ireland to be bound only by laws enacted by their
Parliament, and barring all writs of error or appeals from judgments or decrees in Ireland, to any
Britifh judicature ; and I very much fear there are
men in this-country, who never have forgiven Lord
Buckingham

Buckingham for the part which he took, in advising
a meafure fo neceffary to the peace of Great Britain
and Ireland. It might reafonably have been expected that the people of Ireland, being gratified on the
point of renunciation would have taken breath, and
fufpended at leaft their conftitutional labours. But
the moment the act of renunciation was obtained, a
new grievance occurred, and it was difcovered that
in order to fecure the new conftitution of Ireland,
it was neceffary to alter the frame of the reprefentative body by which in effect it had been eftablifhed ;
and the people being then felf-arrayed and armed,
after due deliberation, it was determined to elect a .
military convention to meet in the metropolis, as
the fureft, moft efficacious, and conftitutional or-
gan, through which to convey the fenfe of the nation upon the fubject of parliamentary reform. This
Convention affembled with confiderable military
pomp and parade at the City of Dublin, and having
affumed to itfelf all the forms and functions of a
Houfe of Parliament, a bill for the reform of the
reprefentation of the people was regularly prefented, read a firft and fecond time, committed, reported, and agreed to, and being engroffed, was
fent at the point of the bayonet by two members of
the Convention, who were alfo members of the
Houfe of Commons, to be regiftered by that affembly. The Houfe of Commons treated this infult
with the indignant contempt which it merited, and
the men who had been betrayed into fuch an act of
contumacious folly awed by the rebuke which they
received

received from the Houfe of Commons, and by the firmnefs of Lord Northington, difperfed and return-ed to the places from whence they, had come, many of them much afhamed of their rafhnefs and intem-perance. And be it alfo · remembered, that one of the loudeft modern declaimers in the Britifh Parlia-ment for Irifh emancipation, was then a Cabinet Minifter of Great Britain, and that he did *then*, with all the energy and ability which diftinguifh him, moft emphatically ftate his opinion to Lord Northington, that the exiftence of legitimate gc-vernment in Ireland, depended on the difperfion of this Convention, and that her connection with the Britifh Crown depended on preferving the frame of the Irifh Houfe of Commons as it then ftood, unal-tered and unimpaired. After the difperfion of this Military Convention, we had a fhort refpite from popular ferment on the ground of conftitutional grievances, but a new topic of difcontent was ftart-ed. It was difcovered that the manufactures of Great Britain were imported into this country upon terms which gave them a preference in the Irifh market,—a preference by the way which fuperior excellence alone can give them, and the remedy pro-pofed for this grievance was, that we fhould com-mence a war of prohibitory duties, although it was notorious that the balance of trade between Great Britain and Ireland was very confiderably in our fa-vour, and that if the Parliament of Ireland had been fo infatuated as to yield to popular outcry upon this fubject, we had not the means of manufacturing

woollen

woollen cloth in this country, nearly fufficient for the ufe of its inhabitants. The difcuffion of this queftion, however, led to the memorable treaty in 1785, if I may fo call it, between the Parliaments of both countries, for a final adjuftment of the com- mercial intercourfe between this country and Great Britain, and the Britifh colonies and plantations, when a fair and liberal offer was made by Great Bri- tain to open her markets, and to fhare her capital with this country; to give to Ireland a perpetual right of trading with her colonies and plantations upon the terms only of our adopting the laws which fhe enacts for regulating her navigation and trade with them. This offer was wifely rejected by the Irifh Houfe of Commons, under a filly deception put upon the people of Ireland, who were taught to believe, that the offer thus made to them was an in- fidious artifice of the Britifh Minifter to revive the legiflative authority of the Britifh Parliament, which had been* fo recently and unequivocally renounced, and under this grofs and palpable deception were the folid interefts of Great Britain and Ireland, their mutual peace and harmony, and indiffolvable con- - nection facrificed in the Houfe of Commons of Ire- land, on the altar of Britifh and Irifh faction. If any thing could have opened the eyes of the nation what paffed within two Seffions from 1785, ought to have expofed the dupery practifed upon them at that period. In the interval, Great Britain thought it neceffary to extend the principle of her navigation acts to fhips Britifh and Irifh built; and in 1787,

the

the Parliament of Ireland did without hefitation adopt this new act of navigation, and declared all the former Britifh acts of navigation to be of force in this country, a point which fome perfons had before that time affected to queftion. And there is no real friend of Ireland who can doubt that it is her intereft to follow Great Britain in her code of Navigation Laws; there is no real friend of Ireland who can doubt that it is her intereft to follow Great Britain in her Code of Laws for regulating her trade with the Britifh colonies and plantations, for on no other terms can we be permitted to trade with them. There muft be one fyftem of imperial policy throughout the Britifh empire, and if we are to remain a part of it, it is idle to fuppofe that the Parliament of Ireland can ever enact laws in oppofition to any principle of imperial policy adopted by Great Britain.

Unhappily in 1789, a new occafion arofe upon which the Parliament of this country thought fit to act upon the moft critical imperial queftion which could have arifen, not only without regard to what had paffed upon the fame fubject in Great Britain, but with direct and avowed hoftility to the Parliament and Government of that country. I pafs by the events of that difaftrous period, and fhall only fay, that the intemperate, illegal, and precipitate conduct of the Irifh Houfe of Commons upon that critical and momentous occafion, has, in my opinion, in all its confequences, fhaken to its foundations our boafted conftitution, and eminently contributed to bring this

country

country into its prefent dangerous and alarming fituation. It is in the recollection of us all, that at the conclufion of the feffion of 1789, nothing was left untried by Lord Buckingham to reftore peace, and to conciliate thofe who had acted with marked perfonal hoftility to him, fo far as he could go without a breach of public duty. If he was capable of harbouring private refentment for unprovoked perfonal injuries offered to him, he had the magninimity to facrifice his feelings to an anxious folicitude for the peace of Ireland; and I have often lamented that his efforts proved unfuccefsful, and that he was compelled much againft his will, to difplace fome old fervants of the Crown who had oppofed his Government with warmth, and not only avowed their determination to perfift in the fame oppofition, but declined with fullen indignation even to hold communication with him. And if the confidential fervants of the Crown are to oppofe his Majefty's Government, and to decline all communication with his Minifters, I am at a lofs to know how it can exift. The firft ftep which was taken in confequence of this political fchifm by gentlemen who had been the fole authors of it, was to found a political club for the reformation of alledged public abufes and political grievances. The firft fociety of that clafs which I believe had exifted in this country; certainly it is the firft within my memory. This political inftitution was announced to the world by a manifefto figned and counterfigned, in which the Britifh Government was charged in direct terms with a deliberate

berate and fyftematic confpiracy to fubvert the liberties of Ireland. The bafis of it was, a folemn refolution to preferve the conftitution of the realm as fettled by the revolution in Great Britain and Ireland in 1688, and re-eftablifhed in Ireland in 1782; and all perfons of congenial fentiments and principles were invited to repair to the ftandard thus raifed for the protection of the conftitution as fettled by the revolution of 1688. The public meafures propofed by this fociety in this their firft manifefto were, as I recollect, a place bill, a penfion bill, and what was called a refponfibility bill; meafures which I have feen refifted warmly by fome members of this fociety when I fat in the Houfe of Commons. In the fucceeding feffions of Parliament, they were brought forward fucceffively and repeatedly, and were fucceffively and repeatedly rejected; the place bill then propofed, was nearly a tranfcript of that which has fince been adopted; the penfion bill authorifed an application of eghty thoufand pounds yearly by the Crown to penfions; and would if then adopted, have been the fole appropriation of the Public Revenue in Ireland; and the refponfibility bill, as it was called, would have conftituted an executive directory, by erecting a commiffion compofed of five public officers, with full power to controul the Crown in the exercife of its vital functions; but in difcuffing the merits of thefe bills, the debates of the Houfe of Commons were conducted with a degree of heat and acrimony utterly unbecoming the gravity and decorum of a legiflative affembly. If we are to credit

dit the Newfpaper reports of the debates which
were carried on in that Houfe at this period, they
exhibit a feries of coarfe and acrimonious, and difgufting invective, fuited only to the meridian of
Billingfgate, and difplayed to the people a picture
of their reprefentatives from their own pencil, little
calculated to infpire them with confidence or refpect. What was the confequence? The people
foon fubfcribed to the opinions which their Reprefentatives had promulgated, and gave them all full
credit for the villainous charges which they had
advanced againft each other; they had been taught
to believe, as often as the political views of contending parties were anfwered by the fuggeftion,
that Great Britain was the natural rival and enemy of this country; that fhe was infincere in all
the conceffions which had been made to Ireland,
and waited only an opportunity to recal them.
That our connection with the Britifh Crown was
a fource of national depreffion, and finally that
a deliberate and fyftematic confpiracy had been
formed by the Britifh Government to fubvert
the liberties of the Irifh nation. For the truth
of thefe affertions let me refer every difpaffi-
onate man to the detail with which I have already troubled your Lordfhips, and for their
wifdom, to fubfequent events intimately connected with them;—to a felf-degraded Houfe of
Commons the people were not likely to appeal for
relief, againft a deliberate and fyftematick Britifh
confpiracy, formed to fubvert their liberties. In a
political

political club compofed of fome of the leading
members of that affembly, they could not be fuppofed very forward to put implicit confidence, and
therefore, with minds enflamed againft the Britifh
name and nation, they looked to political clubs of
their own ; not to procure a place bill, or a penfion
bill, or a refponfibility bill, but to cut off the
fource of all paft and future aggreffions, by fubverting the monarchy, and feparating this country for
ever from Great Britain. The corner ftones of this
wife and falutary projeƈt were, " Catholic Emanci-
" pation and Parliamentary Reform ;" which with
a little foreign affiftance, when the country fhould
be ripe for it, it was hoped, would infallibly enfure
its fuccefs. Accordingly in the year 1791, a new
political club was formed in the metropolis, conneƈt-
ed at its inftitution with fimilar affiliated clubs at
Belfaft and Cork, which was alfo announced by a
manifefto direƈted, not againft Britifh minifters, but
againft the Britifh nation, ftating what was felt as
the real grievance of Ireland, and known to be its
effeƈtual remedy, " That Ireland had no national
government, that fhe was ruled by Englifhmen and
the fervants of Englifhmen ; filled in commerce and
politicks with the narrow prejudices of their country." This is the grievance ; now mark the remedy.—After fcouting the meafure of place bill, refponfibility bill and penfion bill as utterly inadequate
to the difeafe, they refolve that to cut it up by the
root, the reprefentation of the people muft be re-
formed by a general extenfion of 'the eleƈtive fran-
chife

cause, and that a general union amongst *all* the people was effentially neceffary to counteract the weight of Britifh influence. To effect which Union againft Great Britain, an abolition of all religious diftinctions in the ftate was indifpenfible.——An appeal followed to the volunteers of Ireland, befeeching them to refume their arms, and to eftablifh in fact, as they had in theory reftored, the independence of Ireland, and a general recommendation to form fimilar focieties in every quarter of the kingdom, for the promotion of conftitutional knowledge, and the diffemination of *genuine* whig principles. The object of this political affociation feems to be une-quivocally avowed in this their firft manifefto. However a full explanation of it by the author has been twice verified on oath before a fecret committee of this Houfe; in which it is diftinctly avowed that this Irifh Union was originally projected by Mr. Tone, who is now a fugitive for treafon, for the fole purpofe of feparating this kingdom from the Britifh crown ; and the fame project is even more diftinctly avowed in the paper quoted by the noble Baron who fpoke fecond in the debate. Immediately a ge-neral outcry was raifed of commiferation and love for the Catholics of Ireland ; in which for the firft time fince the Reformation a great body of the Proteftant Diffenters joined ; and Catholic Emanci-pation and Parliamentary Reform went forth as the watch words of innovation and treafon ; and the fyftem of innovation and treafon has been purfued from that time, I am forry to fay with equal affiduity

and

and success. I have often lamented that this nest of conspirators calling themselves United Irishmen was suffered to establish itself unmolested in the metropolis; and that the magistrates of the city of Dublin so long delayed any interposition on their part to relieve the Community from such a nuisance. If they had been dispersed on their first appearance, much public mischief would have beeen prevented. The first object of this Jacobin institution was, to detach the Catholics of Ireland from a committee composed of the principal noblemen and gentlemen of their communion, and to place them under the management of a Directory composed of men of a very different description. They saw that so long as the great body of Catholics were directed by men of rank and fortune and approved loyalty, their allegiance had remained unquestioned; and that under such influence, it would be a vain attempt to shake it. Your Lordships well recollect the gross and unpardonable ribaldry with which the public prints teemed against the late Lord Kenmare at the suit of this new Directory, for no other reason than that he had presumed to disapprove a tone of jacobinism and disloyalty which they had assumed, and would have induced them to prefer their claims, in terms of duty and respect to the Legislature Under this Directory a complete system of Democracy was established for the Government of the Catholics of Ireland, and through the mediation of Mr. Tone and his Jacobin associates at Belfast, an alliance was negociated with the Dissenters of the northern

province,

province, who were given to underftand that for concurrence in the fyftem of religious Emancipation, they might expeɛt cordial and decifive fupport from the b ɔdy of the Catholics in the grand projeɛt of Parliamentary Reform, or in other words, of Anarchy and Democracy. To forward this projeɛt, the lower orders of the Catholics were ftimulated to affociate under the title of Defenders, and were impreffed with an opinion, that by robbing the houfes of Proteftants of arms and ammunition, they would contribute to the fuccefs of the Catholic caufe, and finally be relieved from the payment of tythes, taxes and rent. I will not fay that this fyftem of robbery and outrage which was ftruck out for an ignorant and deluded populace, was firft devifed by the Catholic Direɛtory. But your Lordfhips are in poffeffion of full proof, that fome of the unfortunate men who were capitally indiɛted as Defenders n the fummer 1792, were patronized and proteɛted by them, and that confiderable fums of money were paid out of their ftock purfe to defray the expence attending the tryals of fome perfons who were then conviɛted in the county of Louth. For this I have only to refer to the official letter of their fecretary, which was proved before the fecret committee of this Houfe in 1793, and it is ftated at length in their report which has been juft now read *. It is now fully afcertained that a clofe connexion and correfponddence eftablifhed between the Catholic Direɛtory and the Irifh Union.

In addition to this force of midnight robbery and outrage, orders were iffued by the Jacobin Clubs at
Dublin

* See Appendix.

Dublin and Belfaſt, to levy regiments of National Guards in every part of the kingdom; their uniform French, and all their enſigns emblems of diſaffection. This banditti, however, was put down at the firſt moment of its appearance, and I cannot but lament, that every other rebellious combination has not been met with equal vigour and deciſion—If it had—much public miſchief would have been prevented.—The noble Lord who is ſo forward to impute Iriſh diſaffection to what he calls a ſyſtem of coercion, acted upon by the Iriſh Government, and encouraged by the Britiſh Cabinet, will here pleaſe to recollect, that the ſyſtem of midnight robbery and avowed rebellion was completely eſtabliſhed before any one ſtatute was enacted here, to which alone every profligate innovator in Great Britain and Ireland pretends to aſcribe the preſent matured ſyſtem of Iriſh treaſon : and he will alſo pleaſe to recollect, that the firſt of theſe ſtatutes was enacted in conſequence of a Report of a Committee of this Houſe which has been juſt now read; a Committee appointed on the motion of a noble Earl unconnected with Government, and without communication with Lord Weſtmorland, who was then Lord Lieutenant of Ireland; and I lament that a ſevere accident has prevented that noble Earl from attending his duty on this night. It is ſtated diſtinctly in that Report, that in 1792, and 1793, the project of levying a revolutionary army had been formed ; that ſoldiers were forth-coming in abundance, but that officers were wanting; and I will tell that noble Lord, that this

K   project

project was difclofed by evidence the moft clear and fatisfactory, by the teftimony of gentlemen of rank and character, fome of them at this moment high in military command in the King's fervice. The firft act which paffed in confequence of this Report extended only to prohibit the importation of arms and ammunition, or the removal of either by coaft or inland carriage, without licenfe : and will the noble Lord venture, in this affembly, to condemn this wholefome and neceffary meafure of precaution by the Irifh Legiflature, when it appeared diftinctly, that a traiterous confpiracy had been formed in the bofom of their country to levy an army, for the avowed purpofe of overawing and fubverting the conftituted authorities of the ftate. In the fame feffion, in confequence of the fame Report, another act paffed for ftopping the contraband trade of Parliament, for declaring the law with refpect to popular Conventions ; for declaring the law, which I affert with confidence, prohibits and condemns all fuch meetings as unlawful affemblies, tending to difturb public tranquillity, and to raife well-founded alarms in the minds of the King's peaceable fubjects. One of thefe Conventions had recently held a regular feffion in the metropolis, and I have feldom read more feditious and inflammatory libels than were daily circulated in the public prints appointed by authority to report their debates ; and a mandate was actually iffued, early in the year 1793 to elect a National Convention to be holden at Athlone, for the redrefs of national grievances civil and religious.

The

The mode of election was formed by the Irish Union on the model devifed by their jacobin affociates in France : primary affemblies were convened in every parifh to chufe a certain number of electors, who were to meet at a central point in the county, to chufe their reprefentatives. It is not a ftrained inference to fuppofe, that thefe primary affemblies were not attended by the moft fober and induftrious inhabitants of the parifh, and that fobriety and induftry had no very decided influence in the choice of electors; neither does it require any great political fagacity to fee, that if an affembly fo conftituted had been fuffered to eftablifh itfelf, a prompt and general chain of intercourfe and communication would at once have been formed between the turbulent and difaffected members of the community in every part of the kingdom ; and it would have refted with the difcretion of an invifible power, thus poffeffed of the means of receiving and communicating prompt and accurate and general intelligence, to order a general or partial infurrection at pleafure. And yet thefe meafures of Legiflative precaution, thus forced upon Parliament by treafons avowed and meditated, have been reprefented as the original fource of popular difcontent, and have been condemned by the noble Lord in terms of bitternefs and indignation, as a part of the fyftem of coercion as he is pleafed to call it, wantonly inflicted by the Irifh Government upon an innocent and unoffending people, and fecretly encouraged by the Britifh Cabinet. Would the noble Lord be underftood to af-

fert,

fert, that the Irifh Parliament have betrayed their
truft in ftopping the fupply of military ftores to a
revolutionary army, and repreffing tumultuary and
feditious affemblies, notorioufly convened for promoting rebellion, and overthrowing the Conftitution : or would the noble Lord be underftood to infinuate, that the Lords and Commons of Ireland
have betrayed their truft, becaufe they have not
looked at the growth of fedition and treafon tame
and unmoved, in pure compliment to his incre-
dulity. The Parliament of Ireland did their duty in
framing new laws, to meet new and extraordinary
exigencies ; and if there be a ground of cenfure on
Parliament, it is, that their vigour was not propor-
tioned to the magnitude and extent of the evil,
The treafonable affociations which were the fource
of it, were fuffered to augment, unite and marfhal
their difciples, in one common league of mifchief,
infomuch, that under their orders, nearly the whole
of the Northern diftrict, and fome counties conti-
guous to the metropolis, became a fcene of general
murder, and robbery and midnight depredation.
Every man who was accufed by the Brotherhood of
loyalty or peaceable demeanour was ftripped of his
arms—if he prefumed to defend himfelf he was
murdered. The few Magiftrates who ventured to
execute the law, were marked for affaffination, and
many of them were actually murdered : Parliament
therefore found it neceffary to interpofe again,
and to frame a law, if poffible, to meet this
horrid ftate of barbarifm and outrage, which had
bid

bid defiance to the ordinary courfe of juftice; and in the feffion of 1796, the Infurrection Act was paffed, which enables the Lord Lieutenant and Council, on a reprefentation of the Juftices at a Seffion of the Peace, that any particular diftrict is in a ftate of infurrection, by proclamation to declare it fo to be; and the Magiftrates, in a proclaimed diftrict, are enabled to exercife ftrong and fummary powers for reprefling tumult and outrage, and pre-ferving the peace. Amongft others, they are au-thorized to order all perfons within the proclaimed diftrict to remain in their houfes, and to put out their lights after a certain hour of the night. This the noble Lord has been pleafed to reprefent as a re-vival of the obfolete feudal badge of fervitude, the curfew, and a rigorous execution of it throughout the kingdom of Ireland. The firft application to the Lord Lieutenant and Counfel for carrying this act into execution, was made by the magiftrates of the county of Armagh, where a religious feud had broken out, and was attended with lamentable ex-ceffes, a feud which was revived by the wicked ma-chinations of the Irifh brotherhood, and with un-blufhing effrontery reprefented by them, as a Go-vernment perfecution inftituted againft the northern Catholics. I will ftate the fhort hiftory of this reli-gious quarrel, and the noble Lord will fee the griev-ous indifcretion into which he has been betrayed upon this head of his accufation againft the Irifh government. Many years fince the Proteftants, in a mountainous diftrict of the county of Armagh, affociated

affociated under the appellation of Peep of Day
Boys to difarm their Catholic neighbours, who affociated for their common defence under the title of
Defenders. This feud however was foon compofed,
and for years there was not any revival of it; but
when the general fyftem of robbing Proteftants of
their arms was eftabiifhed by the Irifh Union and the
lower order of the Catholics affuming their old ap-
pellations of Defenders, undertook this fervice, the
Proteftants in the county of Armagh affociated for
their common defence under the title of Orange-
men, and feeling in the progrefs of the conteft, that
they were an overmatch for their adverfaries, they
did commit many very grievous exceffes, which I
lament as deeply as the noble Lord. In the origin
of this conteft, many years fince, there is no doubt
the Northern Proteftants were the aggreffors, but
the feud was notorioufly revived by the modern banditti of defenders, who in their turn attacked the
Orange-men, and would have difarmed them. Lord
Camden made every poffible exertion to reftore peace
and to punifh thofe who had violated the law without diftinction. He fent down Colonel Cradock to
take the military force in that diftrict under his
command, with pofitive inftructions to co-operate
with the civil power in fuppreffing tumult, and in
reftoring peace and good order; and fo fenfible were
the gentlemen of the county of Armagh of their
obligations to his Excellency, that at a full meeting
of the magiftrates they returned their thanks unani-
moufly for his extraordinary exertions to maintain
the

the peace of that diftrict. At the enfuing affizes, the Attorney General was fent down with inftructions to profecute indifcriminately every perfon who ftood charged with acts of outrage and difturbance of the public peace, and no man can doubt his impartial difcharge of his duty. But the exertions of the executive government were baffled by the local factions of that diftrict, a general election was at hand, and gentlemen who were candidates for popular favour declined to interpofe between the contending parties, leaft they might impair their election interefts. Under the fame pernicious influence, the Magiftrates of the county were ranged under the banners of Orange-men or Defenders, juft as it beft fuited their election politics, infomuch that if I could have found perfons in that country who would have done their duty, I would have iffued an entire new commiffion of the peace. This is the plain hiftory of the religious feud between the Proteftants and Papifts of the county of Armagh ; a feud which the noble Lord has charged upon the Irifh government as a part of the fyftem adopted for the perfecution of Irifh Catholics, and fecretly encouraged by the Britifh Cabinet,—a perfecution to which, by his account, ninety families had fallen victims on his Lordfhip's eftates.

Let me now ftate the nature of that treafonable combination which has been formed, and which the noble Lord propofes to diffolve by a repeal of the Teft Laws and the act of Supremacy ; a combination the moft dangerous and fingular which is to

be

be found in the annals of the civilized world. The fubordinate focieties confift of thirty members only; when their numbers exceed thirty, the excefs is told off, and a new fociety is founded, with inftructions to make profelytes. And in like manner, whenever their numbers exceed thirty, the excefs becomes the foundation of another club; thefe focieties elect Delegates from each, who form committees of an higher order, which are called Baronial, and have the management and fuperintendance of all the fubordinate clubs or focieties in each Barony; the Baronial committees in like manner elect Delegates in each county, who by the name of county commitees, govern and direct the Baronials. The county committees in like manner elect Delegates, who form a fuperintending provincial committee, for the government and appoint the general executive, whofe ftation is in the metropolis; every member of this union is direction of the feveral county committees in each of the four Provinces; and thefe Provincial Directories bound by folemn and myftic oaths, one of which we know to be, an oath of fecrecy; another, never to give evidence in any court of juftice againft a brother, let his crime be what it may; and a third an oath of fidelity to the French Republic. The refourfes of the union are the feduction of the lower orders of the people, under the fpecious pretext of Freedom and Equality, and every artifice which cunning and profligacy can fuggeft, has been practifed to detach them from the eftablifhed Government.

ment and Conftitution. The PRESS has been ufed
with fignal fuccefs as an engine of rebellion : Sedi-
tion and treafon have been circulated with un-
ceafing induftry, in newfpapers and pamphlets, and
hand-bills and fpeeches, and republican fongs and
political manifeftos. Robbery, affaffination, and maffacre are the efficient powers of the Union, and
are executed with prompt and unerring rigour by
the order of every member of the executive in their
feveral departments. The communication of their
orders is fo managed, as to render detection almoft impoffible. Each fociety has its fecretary
from the general executive, down to the lower
fubordinate clubs, the members of which are generally ufed as the agents of the Union in all acts
of outrage ; and every order is communicated by
the fecretary of the fuperior committee to the fecretary of that committee or fociety, which is next
in immediate fubordination to it ; no fubordinate
committee knows of whom its next fuperior is
compofed ; the accreditted fecretary vouches the
order, from him it is received implicitly, and is
communicated in like manner, 'till it reaches every
member of the union to whom it is addreffed.
The order is generally verbal, but if it be reduced to writing, the moment the perfon who is
to receive and communicate it is fully inftructed,
the paper is deftroyed. Here then is a complete Revolutionary Government organized againft the laws
and eftablifhed conftitution; and let me afk the
noble Lord, whether fuch a combination is to be

L met

met or counteracted, much lefs diffolved by the
flow and technical forms of a regular Government; an invifible power of infinite fubtlety and
extent, which has no fixed or permanent ftation,
which acts by the ungoverned fury of a defperate
and favage race, and fcatters univerfal defolation
and difmay, at its fovereign will and pleafure.
Such was the influence of this fyftem of terror,
that feveral well difpofed perfons were induced
from mere apprehenfions for their perfonal fecurity
to join the union, and fome of them have, I fear,
become reconciled by habit to this general league
of mifchief, under the fame influence witneffes were
deterred from coming forward to give teftimony
for the Crown, and every Juryman who fhould
dare to join in a verdict of conviction was threatened with affaffination. I have read a circular printed
hand-bill wich was publicly diftributed in the difturbed diftricts in the courfe of the laft fummer,
threatening every man who fhould dare to execute
the laws againft a member of the brotherhood with
inevitable deftruction, and in fome counties this
menace had its full effect. Has the noble Lord
heard of the numberlefs murders which have been
perpetrated by the orders of the Irifh union, for
the crime of putting the laws of the country into
a courfe of execution. Has he heard of the murder
of Mr. Butler, a clergyman and a magiftrate? Has
he heard of the murder of Mr. Knipe, a clergyman and a magiftrate? has he heard of the murder
of Mr. Hamilton, a clergyman and a magiftrate,
and

and the circumftances of horror which attended it? This unhappy gentleman who had been a Fellow of Trinity College, and had retired to a college Benefice in the county of Donegall, a man of ex- emplary piety and learning, had been guilty of the heinous crime of inculcating habits of religion and morality and induftry and due fubordination in a wild and remote diftrict; he had alfo been guilty of exertion as a Magiftrate to ftop the pro- grefs of treafon, and was accordingly denounced by the brotherhood. He had, as every other gen- tleman in the fame predicament was obliged to do, converted his dwelling houfe into a fortrefs, which was protected by a military Guard; he had gone to Derry, but hearing of a difturbance in his neighbourhood, he fatally prepared to return and quiet it, intending to take fhelter from his enemies before the return of night. In this, however, he was prevented by a ftorm, which made it impoffible for him to repafs a lake, on the edge of which his dwelling ftood, and he went to the houfe of a friend Mr. Waller, who had been alfo a Fellow of Trinity College, and who to his misfortune received him. Whilft this gentleman and his wife and children were quietly fitting with their gueft by the fire-fide, a volley of mufquetry was difcharged into his houfe, which inftantly killed Mrs. Waller, and this was the firft notice of the attack. The favages who furrounded the houfe cried out for Mr. Hamilton, and threatened to burn it unlefs he was delivered into their hands; when this unfor-

tunate

tunate gentleman was dragged from his hiding place by the fervants of his hoft, delivered into the hands of his enemies, and butchered by them with aggravated circumftances of barbarity too fhocking to relate; his widow and helplefs children have a penfion from the Crown, or they muft have perifh-ed for want. Has the noble Lord heard of the murder of Mr. Cummins, whofe crime was, that he had prefumed to enrol his name in a corps of Yeomanry, under the command of his Landlord, the Earl of Londonderry? Has he heard of the attempt to affaffinate Mr. Johnfton, a magiftrate in the populous town of Lifburn? Has he heard of the recent murder of Colonel St. George, and of his hoft Mr. Uniacke; Has he heard of the recent murder of two dragoons who had difcovered to their officers an attempt to feduce them? In a word, let me afk the noble Lord, whether he has heard of the numberlefs and attrocious deeds of maffacre and affaffination, which form a part of the fyftem acted upon by the Irifh brotherhood, and encouraged by the privileged orders of innovation? I hold the dark and bloody catalogue! but will not proclaim to the civilized world the ftate of cannibal barba-rifm to which my unhappy country has been brought back by thefe peftilent and cowardly trai-tors. Thefe are the men of fentiment whom the noble Lord is anxious to conciliate; thefe are the injured innocents, whofe caufe he has fo often and fo pathetically pleaded; the injured innocents who deal in midnight robbery, conflagration, and mur-der;

der ; and fcatter terror and defolation over the face of his devoted country. The noble Lord may contemplate this fcene of horror with coolnefs from another kingdom, but he will not be furprifed that the gentlemen of Ireland, whofe exiftence is at ftake, do not view it with the fame indifference. I know the noble Lord has declared his opinion that affaffination forms no part of the fyftem which is acted upon by the Irifh brotherhood, and encouraged by the privileged orders of innovation. I know that he has declared his opinion that the numberlefs murders which have been committed in Ireland fince the inftitution of the brotherhood, are but fo many inftances of private and individual fpleen. Nay more, I know the noble Lord has broadly infinuated an opinion, that a periodical paper publifhed in the metropolis, which recommends affaffination, and points out individuals for maffacre, is printed and publifhed by the connivance of the Irifh Government, and forms a part of the fyftem acted upon here and encouraged by the Britifh Cabinet. If the noble Lord continues to hold that opinion, I will for the prefent leave him in the undifturbed poffeffion of it, and fhall only recommend to him to perufe attentively printed reports of the tryal of twelve men convicted of a confpiracy to murder a foldier in the brigade of artillery, who had ventured to reveal to his officers an attempt made to feduce him, and of the tryal of fome domeftics of Lord Carhampton who were convicted of a confpiracy to murder him. If the noble Lord

Lord doubts the authenticity of thefe reports, I beg
to refer him to the'Judges who prefided at the tryals.
When public juftice was thus fubverted ; when the
laws were openly infulted and beaten down ; when
every gentleman who had courage to remain in his
county was marked for affaffination, and had no
protection under his own roof but from a military
guard ; when a plan was actually formed, and nearly ripe for execution, to difarm and cut off the foldiery thus difperfed in fmall bodies for the protection of individuals ; when a fierce and favage foreign enemy hung upon the Irifh coaft, what alternative remained for the Executive Government, but
to furrender at difcretion to a horde of traiterous
barbarians, or to ufe the force entrufted to it for
felf-defence and felf-prefervation ? And what would
have been the folly and debility of the Government,
which could have hefitated to affert itfelf with vigour and decifion at fuch a crifis ? Lord Camden
did not hefitate, but, as became him, iffued an order on the 3d of March, to difarm the rebels in the
Northern diftrict : and if he had not iffued the order, I do not fcruple to fay, that he would have betrayed his truft.   In giving the order, he is fupported by an Addrefs nearly unanimous of both Houfes
of Parliament, and I might reft his juftification on
that Addrefs ; but as the noble Lord has roundly
afferted in another place, that the order iffued by
Lord Camden for difarming the Northern rebels is
given up to be illegal, I now meet him on the point,
and am ready to maintain that the order was, not
only

only ftrictly legal under the circumftances in which
it was iffued ; but that Lord Camden, if he had
with-held it, would have been deeply refponfible for
the mifchiefs which muft have arifen from his omif-
fion. The Conftitution of thefe kingdoms muft be
ftrangely defective indeed if it has not in it a principle of felf-prefervation ; I very well know that it
has no fuch defect, and therefore, when the ordinary
courfe of the municipal law, and the utmoft exertions
of civil magiftrates prove ineffectual for the protection of the Conftitution, and for the fafety and protection of his Majefty's peaceable and loyal fubjects,
it is the bounden duty of the Executive Government to call in the aid of the military power, for
the fuppreffion of treafon and rebellion, and for the
fafety and maintenance of the Conftitution. It was
upon this principle that an order was iffued in 1779,
to the military force of England to act, when the
city of London was attacked by a fanatical banditti,
who had well nigh made themfelves mafters of it.
That order probably faved the Britifh empire ; and
I have no doubt that the order iffued here for difarming the Northern rebels, was effential for the falvation of the kingdom of Ireland. The Minifter who
iffued fuch an order, is deeply refponfible for the act,
if he does it wantonly and on light grounds, he is highly criminal; but if the occafion demands fuch an exertion of authority for the prefervation of the ftate, the
Minifter who with-holds it is refponfible for all the
evil which may arife from fuch an act of timidity :
—of his refponfibility Parliament is to judge :—the
Minifter

Minifter who iffues fuch an order wantonly, or who
with-holds it improperly, is fubject to impeachment;
but the approbation of both Houfes of Parliament
is, by the Conftitution of thefe kingdoms, his full
juftification either for iffuing or withholding the
order. And therefore, I prefume, when the noble
Lord condemned the order iffued by Lord Camden
for difarming the Northern rebels as avowedly illegal, he was not apprized that it received the full,
and nearly unanimous approbation of both Houfes
of Parliament: and, I muft fay, that this is I believe the firft inftance which has occurred in the annals of the Britifh empire, in which the King's Minifter has been called to make his defence for fuppreffing a rebellion ; for iffuing an order, when the
kingdom was threatened with invafion, to feize arms
in the hands of traitors, who waited only to join
the invaders ; arms in which they had no right but
by robbery and treafon, which they ufed in the interval, to terrify the weak into an Union with them,
and to murder every man who had virtue and conftancy to adhere to his allegiance. The noble Lord
has been pleafed on this night to difclaim any charge
of mifconduct by the army in executing this order ;
but in exculpating his brother foldiers he redou-
bles his charge againft the Irifh Government, and
imputes all the affumed mifconduct which he ftated
in another place, to the inftructions given by Lord
Camden to the General Officer who commands in
that diftrict. For the prefent, I pafs by the fingular
apology which he has made for his brother officers,
and

and put it to the noble Lord, why he has ventured to make fuch a random charge againſt the Executive Government, when he might have had precife information on the fubjeƈt, by moving an Addreſs to the Lord Lieutenant, to defire that he would be pleafed to order a copy of thefe inſtruƈtions to be laid on the table. I have a copy of them in my hand, and when the noble Lord hears what they are, he will judge whether the charges which he has hazarded againſt Lord Camden, have a colour of juſtice.—[For Inſtruƈtions, fee Appendix.]

In obedience to thefe orders, General Leake did proceed to difarm the rebels in the Northern diſtriƈt, and executed this fervice with all the moderation, ability and difcretion, which have always marked his charaƈter as a gentleman and an officer ; and in executing this fervice, he did, amongſt others, difarm the rebels of the noble Lord's town of Ballinahinch, which, I am forry to fay, has been for fome years a main-citadel of treafon. In proportion to the fize, it may vie in treafon with the town of Belfaſt. The noble Lord is of a different opinion, and has very fairly affigned his reafons : he fays, that he explained to the tenants in the town and its vicinity the horrors of Republicanifm, the many advantages of the Government and Conſtitution under which they live ; and above all, that he explained to them the fplendid virtues of the Heir Apparent of the crown ; that they all made to him the moſt unbounded profeffions of loyalty, in which however he would not have put implicit confidence, if he had

M   not

not obferved the countenance of every man to whom
he had addreffed himfelf, beam with joy and tri-
umphant affection, when he mentioned the name
and fplendid virtues of his Royal Highnefs the
Prince of Wales. Giving the noble Lord full credit as a phyfiognomift, I muft conclude, if he will
excufe me for a little prefeffional pedantry, that the
loyalty of his town of Ballinahinch is in *abeyance*,
during the life of his prefent Majefty. And, as the
noble Lord has very fairly ftated the grounds of his
opinion, I will as frankly ftate the grounds of mine :
and firft, let me refer the noble Lord to the War-
Office, where he will find minutes of the General
Court Martial, which tried and condemned feveral
foldiers of a regiment of militia, four of whom
were fhot, and he will there find, that thefe unhappy men were feduced into a confpiracy by the people of his town of Ballinahinch, to betray to the
rebels of Belfaft, the military pofts which it was
their duty to defend, and that they were alfo feduced to accept of military commiffions, and military
rank in the revolutionary army of Belfaft and Ballinahinch, which was then organized, and waited only the opportunity to come forth in battle array.
Let me refer the noble Lord to General Leake, for
another proof of loyalty in the town of Ballinahinch ; when he fummoned the inhabitants to deliver up their arms, they refufed to obey him, but on
being threatened with feverity if they perfifted in
this refufal ; they did deliver up their arms, and
amongft other weapons, no inconfiderable number
of

of pikes—are pikes conftitutional arguments for Parliamentary Reform? Are pikes emblems of loyalty? Is the feduction of the King's troops.a fymptom of loyalty? And are thefe the dutiful and affectionate offerings of the noble Lord's tenants and dependents, to the rifing virtues of the Heir Apparent of the crown? Does the noble Lord forget that his domeftics were tainted with the general contagion? That his gardener and groom, in the prefence of Mr. Hamilton, a magiftrate, the noble Lord's manager and agent, acknowledged themfelves to be members of the Union, and acknowledged that pikes and pike-fhafts had been concealed in his timber-yard; and on fearching for them, Mr. Hamilton did frankly confefs his opinion, that they had been removed but the night before General Leake's arrival in the village. The noble Lord will not, I hope, fuppofe me to infinuate that this concealment was made with his knowledge, or countenanced by him. The moft natural place for concealing pikes and pike-fhafts, was the houfe and its appendages of a nobleman in his abfence, whofe fervants and dependents had been feduced into a traiterous confpiracy againft the ftate. His name and rank were very naturally fuppofed to caft a protection around the place of his occafional refidence, and to baffle all fufpicion that it was become a fanctuary of rebellion. The noble Lord ftated, that the imputation of difloyalty on his town of Ballinahinch, refted only on the evidence of a man of the name of Daniel Morgan, whom he reprefents to have been of

infamous

infamous character; but the noble Lord forgot to mention the fate of Morgan. That Daniel Morgan did give an information before one of the Judges of the Court of King's Bench, of treasons committed, and treasons meditated, by many of the inhabitants of Ballinahinch, is most true; it is equally true, that subsequent events have very fully verified every article of his information, and that he was murdered in consequence of the discoveries which he had presumed to make. This unhappy man, after he had sworn his information, went to the town of Downpatrick, and was there protected for some time by a military guard, and having ventured to go into the country at the distance of some miles, on a visit to his wife, who had taken refuge at her father's house, he was murdered there, by a band of ruffians who came on horseback upon this mission; and it was distinctly ascertained, that in the night when this murder was committed, a number of persons had sallied from Ballinahinch on horseback; so that it is at the least highly probable, that the assassins ordered upon this service, were selected from the loyalists of that peaceable town. Within the last two months, under pretence of celebrating the noble Lord's birth-day, the centinels on duty there were made drunk, and this opportunity was taken to rob the King's stores of some hundreds of ball cartridges: such is the state of the noble Lord's town of Ballinahinch, which he has been taught to believe to be a model of sentimental and enthusiastical loyalty; and if he has been so grossly duped and misled

misled in the opinions which he has imbibed of his own immediate tenants and dependents, what must be the extent of his dupery with respect to the county at large?

The noble Lord has thought good on this night to retract the charges originally advanced by him against the army of Ireland, and to declare that the excesses and extravagancies of which he complained, were committed under the direct and immediate orders of the Executive Government. The particular instances of military outrage adduced by the noble Lord were—" The destruction of the printing press of a newspaper, called the Northern Star, at Belfast.—The story of a child in convulsions, whose nurse was ordered to extinguish her lights.—The picketing one, a black-smith, and half-strangling another." As to the first of these charges, in the terms in which it was originally advanced by the noble Lord, an indifferent and uninformed hearer would have imagined, that a regiment headed by its officers had at noon day marched with drums beating and colours flying, under the eye of a General Officer at head-quarters, to demolish the house and the printing-press of a news printer, who had made himself obnoxious to the Executive Government. But what is the fact, of which the noble Lord certainly might have been fully and distinctly apprized? A regiment of militia which I am well informed, until it was cantoned at Belfast and Ballinahinch, was considered as one of the best behaved and best disciplined regiments in the service. had been corrupted

rupted by traitors in both quarters ; feveral of the foldiers had been capitally convicted by the fentence of a General Court Martial, and four of them had been fhot, upon clear evidence that they had yielded to the feduction practiced upon them. The regiment to retrieve its character, fubfcribed to a fund for difcovering and punifhing any new attempt to feduce the foldiery, and made a declaration of determined loyalty to their King and his Government. A body of the foldiers attended by fome non-commiffioned officers not on duty, went to the printer's office to defire that this declaration of loyalty might be printed in his newfpaper, offering to pay for it : he refufed to receive their advertifement, and accompanied his refufal with fome taunting reflections on the foldiers, who did at the inftant, goaded with the recent execution of their companions, which they attributed, perhaps, with fome degree of reafon to the poifon diffufed by the Northern Star, and with the taunting refufal of the Printer to receive the declaration which they would have publifhed, proceed to acts of violence againft him ; and did very nearly deftroy his types and printing prefs; Colonel Leflie, who commanded the regiment, almoft immediately interpofed, brought off his men, and fhut them up in their Barrack ; however, whilft he was thus engaged, another party compofed principally of yeomanry, who were not in uniform, again attacked the Printer's Houfe, and completed the deftruction of his types and printing prefs. Let me afk the noble

Lord

Lord, whether he will venture gravely to affert in this affembly, that he believes this outrage upon military difcipline and the municipal law, to have been contrived and committed under the immediate direction of Lord Camden ; and if he will venture to make the affertion, let me afk him whether I am to underftand his apology for general Lake, and the officers under his command to be, that they have tamely fuffered the King's reprefentative to pafs by them ; and to iffue fecret orders to the foldiery under their command, to go forth as a mob, to the utter fubverfion of military difcipline. Am I to underftand his apology for his brother officers to be, that they hold their military fituations under a government which has maintained a fecret correfpondence and communication with the foldiery under their command, and has ftimulated them to acts of outrage, which the noble Lord did diftinctly in his firft ftatement upon this fubject, infinuate as fcandalous and difgraceful to the military character in Ireland. If this be the noble Lord's apology for General Lake, and for the officers in command in his diftrict, in pure refpect for them, I beg to deprecate it ; and in pure refpect for thefe deferving officers, I beg of the noble Lord to abide by his firft charge againft them however ill founded ; the fecond inftance of military excefs and extravagance, is the rigorous enforcement of that obfolete badge of fervitude the Curfew, " The ftory of the Nurfe and Child ;" I have taken fome pains to come at the truth of this ftory,

ftory, and the refult has been, that I find a light
has been extinguiſhed by order of the officer commanding a patrole in the neighbourhood of Downpatrick, at two different times, and in two different
houfes; both, however, fituated in a proclaimed
diſtrict; in one of tʰefe houfes a child did lay in
convulfions, and it fo happened, that the officer
who commaded the patrole, was alfo the regimen-
tal furgeon; he went into the houfe, and finding
on examination that a child did lay in convulfions,
he fuffered its parents to keep their lights burning,
and early on the next day returned to them for
the purpofe of affording medical affiftance to the
infant. The other inſtance of the enforcement of
the Curfew, happened at the houfe of a man of
the name of Carfon, whofe lights were burning
after eleven o'clock; on being called to by the
patrole to extinguiſh them, and not complying immediately, a foldier broke a pain of glafs in one
of his windows; and fo far was Carfon from com-
plaining of the injury, that he went the next day
to Colonel Bainbridge, who commanded at Downpatrick, and apologized to him for not having aſked
permiſſion to keep his lights burning to fo late an
hour, which had never been denied when he had
applied for it; and it is a fact which I cannot avoid
ſtating, that within the laſt week, Mr. George
Crogier, the noble Lord's land ſteward, and folici-
tor at law, did prefs this fame Mr. Carfon to fur-
niſh him with the particulars which had attended
this grievous enforcement of the Curfew; that
                                                    Carfon

Carfon told him, he had not any ground of complaint, to which Mr. Crogier replied, that unlefs he
would furnifh him with the detail of this military
extravagance, he fhould be dragged to the bar of
the Houfe of Lords, and examined to it on his oath.
So much for the ftory of the nurfe and child—and
now for the ftory of the half ftrangled and picketed
Blackfmith. An information had been made on oath
before Mr. Maxwell, a magiftrate, that a Blackfmith, of the name of Kirke or Shaw, had been employed in making pike-heads, which he had manufactured in great numbers for the rebels in or about
Downpatrick; accordingly Mr. Maxwell went out
with a flank company under the command of a
field officer, to fearch for thefe pike-heads; Mr.
Maxwell apprehended the Blackfmith, who denied pofitively that he had ever manufactured a
fingle pike-head; the ferjeant and fome of the
foldiers put a rope round his neck and drew it
over a beam, in the hope of terrifying him into
a confeffion; but he was not fufpended. The Magiftrate then brought him into the town of Downpatrick, where the Colonel of a Fencible Regiment,
who has died fince, put him on the picket, and he
did immediately difcover the names of feveral
perfons for whom he had manufactured pike-
heads. In confequence of which difcovery, nearly two hundred pikes were feized or brought in
within two days. Let me here requeft of the noble
Lord to reflect on the number of probable murders
which were prevented by this act of military feverity,
and appeal to his candour and good fenfe, whether

N   the

the injury done to fociety in putting Mr. Shaw on
the picket, is in any degree to be put in competition
with the injury which muft have arifen, in leaving
two hundred pikes of his manufacture in the hands
of the rebels and affaffins of that difturbed diftrict.
I deplore as fincerely as the noble Lord can do,
thofe neceffary acts of feverity; but the executive
government was reduced to the painful alternative
of ufing the force entrufted to it in defence of the
King's peaceable and well affected fubjects, or of
tamely giving them up to the fury of a fierce and favage democracy. Every man of feeling muft lament
the painful duties which we impofed on military
officers employed in the fuppreffion of a rebellion.
The noble Lord was employed on this fervice in
America, where he was reduced to the painful, but
I am confident the indifpenfable duty of ordering a
gentleman who bore the commiffion of a Colonel, to
fummary execution, without the formality of a trial.
He will readily perceive that I allude to the cafe of
Colonel Ifaac Haynes, who was hanged at Charleftown in the year 1781. This gentleman had taken
the oath of allegiance to his Majefty, and was fuffered to retire to his plantation fome miles up the
country; the ufe which he made of this indulgence
was, to excite fedition, difaffection, and difturbance
in the adjacent diftrict, to terrify the weak and timid
into an Union with him, and to murder every man
who had conftancy to refift his folicitations. Of this
defcription was an Irifhman of the name of Creighton, whofe houfe he furrounded with an armed banditti in order to murder him, but Creighton had
time

time to make his efcape to Charleftown; and a patrole having come up with Haynes, and feized him.
On identifying his perfon by a court of enquiry, he
was hanged at Charleftown, by order of the noble
Lord, and of Colonel Balfour. I ftate thefe facts from
the printed Reports of the Debates of the Britifh
Houfe of Lords, in February 1782 : and upon the
fame authority I will ftate, that the defence made
for the noble Lord in that affembly by a near friend
and connection of his was, that the Commander in
Chief had fully approved of the execution of Colonel Haynes, and that fimilar executions had taken
place in hundreds of inftances during the American
war. Let me repeat, that I do not allude to this act
of extreme military feverity in any manner with a
view to condemn it : I am confident that the noble
Lord in iffuing his order, felt that it was an act on
his part of painful and indifpenfible duty;—but
with that feeling in his mind, I cannot but wonder
that the noble Lord has brought forward the ftory
of the curfew, and the ftory of the inquifition, the
ftory of the nurfe and child, and the ftory of the
blackfmith, more efpecially when I recollect the
ftrong comment which the noble Lord has tranfmitted to pofterity, upon a propofed parliamentary enquiry into the execution of Colonel Haynes, as an
unpardonable abufe, in his opinion, of parliamentary privilege and authority. Soon after Lord Camden had iffued his order for difarming the rebels in
the northern diftrict, he was enabled to come at evidence the moft diftinct and fatisfactory of the fyftem
of treafon eftablifhed by the Irifh brotherhood, and
the

the means by which this difcovery was made were
purely accidental. A man of the name of Newell,
an United Irifhman, by profeffion a portrait pain-
tor, had been a member of one of the fuperior
committees of the brotherhood ; he had gone to the
houfe of a gentleman in the county of Down, whofe
loyalty was unqueftioned, to draw portraits of fome
of his family, and being prevented by ficknefs from
attending his committee of the brotherhood for
more than a fortnight, he was immediately fufpected of having betrayed the fecrets of the brotherhood
to his employer, and marked accordingly for affaffination. An attempt was made to execute this fentence upon him by night in the town of Belfaft,
when finding himfelf denounced, he did give information which enabled the executive government to
feize three committees, with all their papers, in the
very act of traiterous council. Thefe papers were referred to fecret committees of both Houfes of Parliament, and the noble Lord acknowledges that he has
read the reports made by them, but he has this night
pretty plainly infinuated, that he confiders the committees who made their reports, and the two houfes
who concurred with them, to be little fhort of dupes
and drivellers, inafmuch as he has difcovered, by a
confeffion made by Newell and by another man of the
name of Smith, which he has read fince his laft
arrival in Ireland, that the evidence given by both
is falfe and fabricated. Let me afk the noble Lord
whether he has been favoured with the confeffion of
the worthy gentlemen who bribed this fmith and
Newell to make fuch a declaration ? Has the gentleman,

man, who paid each of them a fum of 400l. favoured the noble Lord with a detailed account of that
tranfaction? And has Mr. Newell fatisfied the noble
Lord by his confeffion, that the papers feized at
Belfaft, and referred to both Houfes of Parliament,
are alfo falfe and fabricated? Has Mr. Newell's confeffion, which the noble Lord has read fatisfied him,
that the official returns of cannon, and mufquets, and
military ftores, of foldiers organized for a revolutionary army; the official plan of a revolutionary committee; the projected fcheme of maffacre and con-
fifcation, all reduced to writing, and feized upon
three diftinct committees of treafon fitting in council, are fiction and fabrication. Has Mr. Neville's
confeffion which the noble Lord has read fince his laft
arrival in Ireland, fatisfied him that the report of the
committee of this Houfe, ftating that it appeared
diftinctly to them that the ambaffador had been fent
from hence by the brotherhood in the year 1795, to
treat with the executive directory of the French
Republic, is alfo mere fiction and delufion? And
will the noble Lord gravely infinuate, that the
Lords and Commons of Ireland are dupes and drivellers? And that the noble Lord, by his refidence
in another country, or by his occafional vifits in
Ireland, where he is furrounded by men who are
anxious to deceive him, is now enabled to correct
their errors and delufions? With all refpect to
the noble Lord it is an affumption, on his part,
to which I muft take leave to enter my proteft; and
I doubt not I fhall be joined by a very great majority
indeed of the gentlemen who feel a permanent in-

tereft

tereft in the fafety of this country. When upon
the reports made to both Houfes of Parliament, they
voted a joint and unanimous Addrefs to the Lord
Lieutenant, defiring that he would exert the whole
energy of the powers civil and military entrufted to
him for the fuppreffion of exifting rebellion; and in
confequence of this Addrefs, his Excellency did,
with the advice and concurrence of his Privy Council, iffue a Proclamation notifying to all his Majefty's
fubjects, that he had in purfuance of the joint Addrefs of both Houfes of Parliament, iffued his orders to all executive officers civil and military to maintain the public peace, and to fupprefs treafon, rebellion
and infurrection; and in the body of this proclamation, his Excellency did offer full pardon and indemnity
to all perfons who fhould within a reafonable time,
I think fix weeks, return to their allegiance; and
the term for coming in was extended by a fubfequent
proclamation, I think to fix weeks more. The noble Lord will not, I am confident, condemn a proclamation here, thus iffued under the authority of
both Houfes of Parliament, and I truft he will not
condemn it a fecond time in another place. And
when the noble Lord was pleafed on this night to
impute fome of the exceffes of which he complained, to the orders or inftructions given to the Commander in Chief by Lord Camden, I muft again
ftate to him my furprize that he fhould make fuch a
vague and random charge againft his Excellency,
when he might have had precife and accurate information on the fubject, by moving for a copy of the
inftructions. I have in my hand a copy of Lord
Camden's

Camden's inſtructions to the Commander in Chief, and of his general order iſſued in purſuance of them, which I will alſo read to the noble Lord.—(Here he read them, for which ſee Appendix.)

The vigorous meaſures adopted by Lord Camden, in which he was ſo fully ſupported by both Houſes of Parliament, had in a great meaſure ſtopped the progreſs of rebellion, when it was again ſet into motion by a moſt prepoſterous proceeding, inſtituted by ſome gentlemen of rank and fortune in the county of Down. Early in the laſt Summer, it was reported that a change of Britiſh miniſters was in agitation, and I have been well informed that a let-ter from a nobleman, who it was ſuppoſed would take a lead in the new Cabinet, was read at a tavern in this town to a motley aſſembly of United Iriſhmen and others, exhorting them to ſet the people of Ireland to work in the way of addreſſes to his Ma-jeſty, for that the critical time had arrived when the ſupport of the new embrio Cabinet was eſſential. And at this critical time, when the whole of the county of Down was proclaimed by law to be in a ſtate of inſurrection, and when it had recently been a general ſcene of midnight robbery, conflagration and murder, an advertiſement appeared in the pub-lic prints, calling on the High Sheriff to convene the inhabitants of the county without diſtinction, whether inſurgents or not, to meet, in order to frame a petition to his Majeſty for the diſmiſſal of his Miniſters; and what ſeems ſcarcely credible, amongſt the perſons who ſigned this curious requiſi-tion to the Sderiff, were the names of ſome Magiſ-

trates

trates who firſt memorialed the Lord Lieutenaut and
Council to proclaim the county under the infurrec-
tiou act, as was the name of a Reverend Prelate,
who I fee in hïs place on this night, for the firſt
time that he has appeared there for years. The
High Sheriff, much to his credit, refuſed to comply
with this monſtrous requiſition made to him to collect the infurgents of the county of Down by colour
of his authority ; and the gentlemen who had formed this project for bringing together a body of ten
or twenty thouſand of them, gave it up, as they
profeſſed, only from an apprehenſion that ſuch a
tumultuous affembly would have been difperfed by
the Magiſtrates. But the petition was framed, and,
if I have been well informed, that Reverend Prelate
not only ſigned it, but did without referve folicit fignatures to it ; and if I have been well informed, a
clergyman of the eſtabliſhed Church, a member of the
Chapter of the Cathedral of Down, did read this petition fromthe pulpit in a Diffenter's Meeting-houfe,
and publicly folicit his auditory to put their names to it.
I mention this circumſtance in the hearing of that
Reverend Prelate, that he may enquire into it at his
next viſitation, and if he finds that ſuch an act of
profane indecorum was committed by a member of
his Chapter, he may inflict a cenfure upon him ade-
quate to his offence. This petition has appeared in
all the public prints ; it fets out by a complaint that
the war and the mifconduct of Miniſters have de-
ſtroyed the manufactures and the trade of that diftrict. It is a difcovery referved for that fagacious
prelate, and his more fagacious compeers, that a

war

war which has ravaged the German empire muft
leffen the demand for Irifh linens. But how does
the fact bear them out in this affertion? The value of
linens exported from Ireland in the four years prior
to the war, from 1788, to 1791, inclufive, is nine
millions four hundred and fifty-eight thoufand two
hundred and ten pounds, and the value for the four
fubfequent years, from 1792, to 1795, inclufive, is
eleven millions fix hundred and fixty-two thoufand
one hundred and fifty-five pounds ; fo that it appears diftinctly, that in the four firft years of the
war the linen manufacture, the ftaple of Ireland,
and the only manufacture of the Northern diftrict,
has encreafed to the amount in value of more than
two millions two hundred thoufand pounds, over
and above the amount of it in the four correfponding years prior to the war ; and in the year 1796,
which I have not taken into this calculation, the
value of linen exported, was three millions one hundred and thirteen thoufand, fix hundred and eighty-
feven pounds, a fum infinitely greater than the export
had ever before amounted to in any one year, fince the
linen manufacture was firft eftablifhed in Ireland. So
much for the veracity of that Reverend Prelate,
and his co-petitioners in this firft affertion carried
by them to the foot of the Throne. It is perfectly
true, that in the laft year, (1797) the export of
linen fell above ten millions of yards ; but if that
Right Rev. Prelate and his compeers, had thought
fit to ftate truth to his Majefty, they would have
ftated, that the linen weavers of the county of
Down, had altogether deferted their looms, and

O addicted

addicted themfelves to politics, they would have ftated to his Majefty that they had exchanged their Shuttles for Pikes and mufkets and cannon; that their nights-were devoted to every fpecies of excefs and outrage, and therefore, that a total ftop was put to fober and honeft exertion amongft the lower order of the people; and if the Right Rev. Prelate and his compeers had told truth to his Majefty, they would have ftated, that their petition, fraught as it is with virulent falfehood and mifreprefentation, had been hawked about the country for the mifcievous purpofe of enflaming the minds of the people, and of diverting them from habits of fober induftry and fubmiffion to the laws, and that this wife and patriotic effort has had its full effect. With equal veracity it is ftated to his Majefty, that the commerce of that diftrict has been annihilated by the war and by the mifconduct of Minifters; how does the fact bear them out in this affertion? By official returns from the commiffioners of the cuftoms it appears, that the cuftoms of the port of Belfaft, for the four years of the war compared with the four correfponding years prior to it, have not fallen, on an average, quite feven thoufand pounds a year; although the importation of foreign fpirits has almoft wholly ceafed, and although it is perfectly notorious, that fince the year 1791, the town of Belfaft has been a citidal of treafon, a circumftance not much in favour of its credit in foreign countries; perhaps the Right Rev. Prelate will tell me that the reprefentation to his Majefty went not to any particular diftrict, but

to

to the kingdom at large; here again I meet him
with official documents, from which it appears that
on a comparative view of the trade of Ireland, exports and imports, during eight years, ended at
Lady-day 1797, there is an accruing ballance in
her favour of more than fix millions five hundred
and forty thoufand pounds; and the increafe of
her tonnage has been feventeen thoufand eight
hundred feventy-two tons in the fame period.
This is the country, whofe trade and manufactures
the Right Rev. Prelate reprefents to his fovereign,
as annihilated by the war and by the mifconduct of
minifters; this is the country which he reprefents,
to his fovereign as finking under the weight of
mifgovernment; this is the country which his fovereign is to refcue from impending ruin only,
by a radical parliamentary reform. But what
will that Right Rev. Prelate fay for himfelf in
having joined in a reprefentation to his Majefty,
that the *moſt conſtitutional and loyal means of feeking redrefs*, have been oppofed by the moſt conſtitutional and illegal coercions. What will that
Right Reverend Prelate, a Bifhop of the eftablifhed
Church, fay for himfelf, in having thus juftified to
his flock an organized fyftem of murder and robbery, and midnight conflagration, as the moſt uncon-
ftitutional and loyal means of feeking redrefs, and
in approaching his Sovereign with this premeditated
and unblufhing impofition. And is there falvation
for a country, in which gentlemen of rank and fortune, headed by a Chriftian Bifhop, can be mifled
into

into fuch acts of criminal folly and levity, not to be-
ftow upon them a harfher epithet. About the fame
period a fimilar act of wifdom was committed in the
county of Kildare, and a fimilar petition was hawked about that county for fignatures, to which it is
faid the name of a mendicant cripple is affixed,
whofe ftation for more than twenty years has been
on the high way at half a miles diftance from Naas,
and who muft be familiar to every gentleman that has
travelled on the fouthern road ; and I have been informed by unqueftioned authority, that a peer of
the realm did fpend an entire day in the little town
of Leixlip foliciting fignatures to this petition, and
that his canvafs was retarded more than an hour by
a blackfmith, who refifted the importunities practifed upon him to forfake his hammer and his anvil,
and to addict himfelf to the politics of his noble
preceptor. What was the confequence of this act
of criminal folly in the county of Kildare? From a
ftate of perfect tranquillity and good order, it became almoft immediately a fcene of general tumult
and outrage, infomuch that the refident gentlemen
were compelled to feek for fafety and protection by
maintaining regular military garrifons in their
houfes, and fortifying every part of them, which
was open to affault, and fuch was the bafe and brutal
fpirit of the infurgents, that their beft benefactors
were marked for deftruction. Mr. Conolly, who
had fpent the whole of his life and a princely fortune
amongft them, who was more than feconded in acts
of unbounded charity and benevolence by that excellent

cellent woman; who, if perfection be the lot of
human nature, is a model of it; who has employed
the whole of her life in administering comfort to the
poor in a district of miles around her, as if they
were members of her family, who has fed the hun-
gry and cloathed the naked, and healed the fick,
and brought up their children in the ways of religion and virtue, and honeft induftry; Mr. Conolly
and this moft excellent lady were marked as the objects of plunder and deftruction, by the wretches
who had exifted for a courfe of more than thirty
years by their bounty. And this gentleman and his
lady, who have thus devoted their lives, and a great
and princely fortune, to acts of unbounded benevolence in a circuit of miles around them, are at this
moment indebted for perfonal fafety in their manfi-
on-houfe, to the protection of a military guard, and
dare not make ufe of the lower apartments in it, under the apprehenfion of a midnight falute of mufquetry. And the noble Lord may reft affured, if
he fhould return to his country refidence in Ireland,
he may meet the fate from the loyalifts of Ballyna-
hinch which was intended for Mr. Conolly by gentlemen of the fame ftamp at Celbridge.

Notwithftanding the patriotic efforts of fome worthy and reverend gentlemen in the county of Down
to perfuade the people that their commerce and manufactures were annihilated, and that the acts of
outrage and rebellion into which they were feduced,
are the moft loyal and conftitutional means of redrefs, order and tranquillity were reftored in the
courfe

courfe of the laft Summer in a confiderable part of
that diftrict; a very great number of deftructive
weapons had been feized and fecured in the King's
ftores. In the county of Down and the adjacent diftrict, more than four thoufand pikes, feveral thoufands of fire-arms, two fmall pieces of cannon and
a howitzer. And in another diftrict, a noble Lord
who fits near me was enabled to feize twelve hundred
pikes and two pieces of cannon, fix-pounders. The
people were returning faft to habits of induftry, and
confidence was fo far reftored, that juftice had in
fome of the difturbed counties refumed its courfe,
infomuch that feveral perfons were capitally convicted of treafon and murder, others of adminiftering
unlawful and treafonable oaths,—amongft the latter
a man of better rank in fociety, of the name of
William Orr. Inftantly a new revolutionary engine
was fet at work, and the adminiftration of juftice
was fyftematically libelled in all its departments;
a newfpaper has been fet up in the metropolis, if
report is to be credited, at the fuit of a young gen-.
tleman who may one day have a feat in this.
Houfe, fyftematically to degrade the adminiftra-.
tion of juftice; and this Mr. William Orr has.
been publickly held out as a martyr, and a victim
facrificed by the Executive Government in violation·
of criminal juftice; and a gentleman, whom I be-.
lieve the people of England have the happinefs to
behold as one of their reprefentatives, has with
equal decency and wifdom, at a late drunken tavern
meeting in another country, given by way of fenti-.
mental

mental toaft, " the memory of William Orr who
was bafely murdered in Ireland;" and his neigh-
bour, not to be outdone in wifdom and difcretion by
this worthy fenator, announced to the chairman his
fentiment, " that the Irifh Cabinet may foon take
the place of Mr. Orr." I have informed myfelf accurately of the circumftances which attended this
unhappy man's conviction, which I will ftate, and
as I ftate them in the hearing of the noble and learned Lord who fat upon his trial, if I fhould commit any the moft trivial miftake, I have no doubt he
will fet me right : he was indicted for adminiftering
an unlawful oath to two foldiers of the names of
Wheatly and Lindfay, an oath certainly intended to
feduce them from their duty ; what led to the difcovery of their feduction was, the feizure of fome
official papers at Londonderry, upon a committee of
United Irifhmen, in which thefe two foldiers were
returned by name by one of their correfponding
committees, as *being up*, which is the cant phrafe of
the brotherhood to defcribe its members : thefe men
were immediately feized by their officers, and examined feparately, and on their examination, they
both agreed in the detail of their evidence, and
having fworn information before a magiftrate againft
Mr. Orr, for adminiftering an oath of feduction to
them, he was arrefted, and brought to trial. On
his trial both the foldiers were examined, and proved
diftinctly, that Orr had adminiftered the oath to
them in the prefence of feveral perfons, whom they
named ; and after a long and puzzling crofs examination,

nation, as I am informed, nothing appeared which could invalidate their teftimony. An attempt was made. by the prifoner, in his defence, to impeach the credit of one of them, I think of Wheatley, in which he failed fo completely, that the learned Lord who prefided at the trial could not even take down this evidence on his note book ; but no attempt whatever was made at or after the trial, to impeach the credit or to invalidate the teftimony of Lindfay ; and although both the foldiers named feveral perfons who had been prefent when they were fworn by the prifoner, not one of them was produced on his part or examined in contradiction of the foldiers. On this evidence the Jury found him guilty, and re- commended him to mercy ; the next day a motion was made in arreft of judgment, and to the fcandal and difgrace of the profeffion to which I belong, in a partial and garbled report of the trial of this un- happy man, which every lawyer who reads it muft fee is the production of a Barrifter, the public are given to underftand that there was but one count in the indictment to which the objection was made in arreft of judgment ; and the public are alfo given to underftand that this unhappy man was tried and convicted under an expired ftatute, although it is clear as any point could be, that the original ftatute would not have expired till the end of this feffion of parliament ; and an act had paffed laft year for explaining and amending it, which is altogether fuppreffed, and although thefe were the counts in the indictment, to all of which the evidence on the

trial

trial equally applied, and two of them were unob-
jected to by the prifoner's council, yet is this circumftance alfo fuppreffed ; and in the fame garbled
and mutilated report, an affidavit of two of the Jurors is printed, that whifkey was introduced into
the jury-room, and that they were drunk when they
gave their verdict, and to the fcandal and difgrace
of an honourable profeflion, in the fame report, one
of the prifoner's counfel is reprefented as having
ftated this affidavit in open Court, on the flimfy pretence of moving the Court of Oyer and Terminer
for an attachment againft thefe Jurymen upon the
voluntary affidavit, which they had been prevailed
upon to make, accufing themfelves of having given
their verdict in a ftate of intoxication ; and in the
fame report a voluntary affidavit of a diffenting
Clergyman, taken moft improperly by a Magiftrate
after Orr's conviction, is alfo printed, in which he
ftates fome time fince he attended Wheatley at the
village of Rafharkin on a fick bed, when he confef-
fed that he had committed a number of crimes, and
amongft others the crime of perjury ; and in the
fame affidavit he defcribes Wheatley pretty plainly
as being in a ftate of mental derangement when he
made this confeffion. On the return of the learned
Lord to town he laid the recommendation of
the Jury before the Lord Lieutenant, and being
afked by his Excellency whether he had a doubt on
his mind of the guilt of Mr. Orr, and whether he
would join in recommending him to mercy ? The
learned Lord declared he had no doubt on his own

P   mind

mind of the guilt of this unhappy man, and that he could not recommend him to mercy confiftently with his duty. His Excellency, notwithftanding this declaration of the learned Lord, refpited Mr. Orr, to give time for enquiry whether any juftifiable ground could be laid for extending mercy to him, and finding that nothing could be fubftantiated to fhake the juftice of his conviction, the unhappy man was left for execution. The affidavits which I have ftated never were laid before the Lord Lieutenant; but if they had, is there a man with a trace of the principles of juftice in his mind, who will fay that fuch affidavits ought to be attended to? Is it to be fuppofed that a Judge would receive a verdict from a Jury in a ftate of intoxication? Or was it ever heard that a Juryman was received, by voluntary af- fidavit, to impeach a verdict in which he had con- curred? Will any man with a trace of criminal juf- tice in his mind fay, that a voluntary affidavit of a perfon not produced, unexamined at the trial, ought to be received after conviction, to impeach the credit of a witnefs who was examined and crofs- examined, and whofe credit ftood unimpeached by legal evidence? If fuch an affidavit were to lay the neceffary foundation of a pardon after conviction, I will venture to fay there is no man who may be convicted hereafter of any crime, however atroci- ous, that will not be able to obtain a fimilar affida- vit. I wifh Magiftrates to know, that in taking fuch affidavits, they are guilty of a grofs breach of duty; they have no jurifdiction or authority to adminifter

voluntary

voluntary oaths or to take voluntary affidavits. The perfon who takes fuch an oath, or makes fuch an affidavit, cannot be convicted of perjury if he fwears falfely ; and, I am forry to fay, that it is no uncommon practice in Magiftrates to fign inftruments which are called affidavits, without obliging the perfons who fign them to make oath as to the truth of their contents. If a doubt could be entertained upon the evidence given on his trial of the guilt of Mr. Orr, his dying declaration feems to me to be a plain confeffion of it ; he is made to declare generally that the foldiers who accufed him were forfworn, but for this general declaration he had this plain fubterfuge,—that *he* had adminiftered an oath to them, not to give evidence againft any brother of the Union. He feems diftinctly to avow the offence of which he was convicted, and to deny the juftice and authority of the ftatute which makes it a-capital crime. The fact is, that this unhappy man was a principal and confidential member of the brotherhood, and his execution was confidered a fatal blow to the caufe of treafon ; and therefore it is that all this outcry has been raifed, in the hope of doing away the effects of fuch an example, and of terrifying judges from difcharging their duty, and the executive Government from prefuming to withhold pardon from any leading member of the brotherhood who may hereafter be convicted. The wretched beings of the inferior orders whom they feduce, are configned to their fate without remorfe or murmur.

Soon

Soon after the execution of Mr. Orr, a moſt attrocious libel was publiſhed on the judge who had
tried him, and on his Excellency the Lord Lieutenant, for ſuffering juſtice to take its courſe ; and a
wretched printer of the name of Finerty, who had
been put forward to ſwear himſelf the ſole proprie-
tor of the newſpaper in which it was publiſhed, was
tried and convicted, and ſentenced to the pillory and
impriſonment on an indictment for the publication :
and in order to do away the effects of this example,
a new expedient was deviſed : a libel infinitely more
flagrant and miſchievous was immediately circulated
in pamphlets, and newſpapers, as the ſpeech of one
of his Majeſty's Council, delivered by way of defence for the printer on his trial : I will not believe
that an honourable profeſſion has been ſcandalized
and degraded, by the delivery of ſuch a farrago of
falſehood and ſedition in a court of juſtice : I will
not believe that any gentleman who wears the gown
of that honourable profeſſion, could be found to inſinuate broadly to the jury, who were to give a verdict on the trial of his client, that they were packed
and garbled, becauſe the ſheriff by whom they were
impannelled derived his authority from the crown :
I will not believe that any gentleman of that honourable profeſſion would venture to ſtate diſtinctly, that
his client could expect from the judge to whom he
addreſſed himſelf, at beſt, but a cold and inanimate
ſtatement of facts, and the law ariſing from them,
thus in plain terms inſinuating, in the true ſpirit of
the brotherhood, that the ſources of criminal juſtice

tice are poifonous and corrupted. No, in their rage for degrading the adminiftration of juftice, they would blaft the chara&er of their retained advocate, by falfely and foully reprefenting him as facrificing his miferable client to the caufe of fedition and trea- fon, and by imputing a libel to him for which the author ought to have accompanied Mr. Fjnerty on the pillory.

I truft the noble Lord has heard enough on this night to open his eyes with refpe& to the ftate of the kingdom of Ireland. But if any thing is wanting to flafh convi&ion on his mind, of the difloyalty and treafon of the Irifh Union, let him look to what is now paffing in the fouthern and midland diftricts; during all the difturbances which prevailed in other parts of the kingdom, we were in a ftate of profound tranquility and contentment there; the farmers had already tafted the fweets of fober induftry; agriculture was encreafing moft ra- pidly, and the country wore the face of wealth, and comfort and happinefs; nay, more, the condi- tion of the loweft order of the peafantry was meli- orated in a degree that I never flattered myfelf I fhould have lived to witnefs; we never heard there of parliamentary reform or Catholic emancipation; and if the noble Lord was to talk of either to a farmer or a peafant of the fouthern or weftern Pro- vince, he would comprehend him as little as he would underftand the quotation from Tully which his Lordfhip has juft now made; when the ene- my appeared on the coaft in the laft year, a gene- ral

ral fentiment of loyalty prevailed in all ranks and degrees of the people, who vied with each other, in contributing to defend their country againft the invaders ; on the report of general Hoche, at his return to France, of this unexpected loyalty in the people of Ireland, the ambaffadors of the Irifh Union refident at Paris, were reproached with having impofed upon the directory, and in confequence of this reproach, inftructions were tranfmitted to the Irifh directory to organize the fouth of Ireland, as they had organized the north ; and accordingly emiffaries have been employed to feduce the people of that diftrict with fo much fuccefs, that there has been a fudden and immediate tranfition in almoft every part of the Province of Munfter, and alfo in many counties in Leinfter, from peace and good order and contentment to general tumult and outrage, and every fpecies of cruelty and barbarifm. Will the noble Lord fay, that the prefent difturbed ftate of the fouthern diftrict is to be imputed to the fyftem of coercion, as he calls it, acted upon by the government of Ireland, and encouraged by the Britifh Cabinet ? Coercion, as he calls it, was never put into practice there, 'till unhappily the recent feduction of the giddy and deluded people of that diftrict compelled the magiftrates and refident gentlemen to fly for refuge to the executive government, and to call for the execution of the infurrection act in their own defence. But I make no doubt that we fhall foon be told by fome of the noble Lord's political friends in Great Britain,

Britain, that the miserable inhabitants of the south of Ireland have been goaded to insurrection by the system of coercion, and that they have only fought for Parliamentary Reform and Catholic Emancipation by the most loyal and constitutional means ; and certainly this story may be told of the people of the south, with the same degree of truth with which it has been propagated by the injured inhabitants of the north. Let me now make a serious and solemn appeal to the noble Lord ; let me call upon him to state distinctly and unequivocally whether he believes there is at this hour an organized and extended system of treason rooted in the kingdom of Ireland ? If he answers that he does not believe it, let me ask him what he considers to be symptoms or proofs of treason ? Does he consider the project of levying a revolutionary army a proof of treason ; does he consider the seduction of the King's troops a proof of treason ; does he consider a conspiracy to seize the King's forts and arsenals a proof of treason. Such a conspiracy was detected within the last month at Athlone. Does he consider the formation of secret depots of arms and ammunition a proof of treason ; does he consider the concealment of cannon as a proof of treason ; does he consider the distribution of pikes amongst the lowest order of the people a proof of treason ; Does the consider the mystick revolutionary Government of the Irish Union as a proof of treason ; does he consider a regular correspondence carried on by the Executive Directory of the Union with the King's enemies to be a proof of treason.

The

The fact is so notorious that I must suppose the noble Lord has heard that there now is and has been for a considerable time an accredited minister plenipotentiary of the Irish Directory resident at Paris; a man who received the rudiments of his education in a seminary of Jesuits, and completed it in the office of an Attorney at Law. The noble Lord has I presume also heard that the Irish Directory had three accredited ministers resident at Lisle during the late negociation for peace, to counteract the King's minister Lord Malmesbury. I make no doubt the noble Lord would recognize these gentlemen if he were to hear their names, as they are all natives of Belfast. And let me ask the noble Lord whether he has come express to this kingdom, seriously to recommend to us to oppose conciliation to rebellion, to oppose cannon pikes with conceffion and sentiment and romance and fine feeling. If the noble Lord had been so opposed in America, there can be no doubt what would have been the event of his campaigns. But if the noble Lord has so much confidence in conciliation, he certainly has not commenced his operations with judgment, he should have set out by making his proposition to the Directory of the Union; and first let me ask him whether he knows of whom the Directory is composed; if he does, he will do a very signal service to the nation by disclosing their names. I suspect very strongly that the noble Lord has seen and communicated with some of them since his last arrival in Ireland; not officially as members of the Directory, for I am

pretty

pretty confident they would feel the fame reluctance in community officially with the noble Lord, that they would feel in community with me; but as members of the head committee of grievances appointed to collect materials for this long expected debate. I am apt to fufpect that fome of the Directory may have tendered their fervices to the noble Lord. If they will negociate with him, he will find the event to be that we fhall be defired by way of preliminary to lay down our arms, to reftore to the Union all the arms and ammunition which we have taken from them, to repeal the teft laws and the act of fupremacy, and to give them a Democratic Houfe of Commons upon the bafis of general fuffrage, and when the preliminaries are conceded, in the true fpirit of their brethren of France, they will tell us what further conceffions they may have to demand.

I fear I have exhaufted your Lordfhips' patience, and I have very nearly exhaufted my ftrength. But before I fit down I muft very fhortly advert to the fyftem of conciliation which the noble Lord has recommended, and firft to the fyftem of Emancipation; A phrafe I muft fay of equal wickednefs and folly when applied to any clafs of his Majefty's fubjects in this kingdom. Does the noble Lord know that the whole code of the popery laws enacted fince the Revolution has been repealed ; and that there is not at this hour a fingle difability affecting a Papift or Roman Catholic fave one, that is a reftriction in the ufe of fire-arms to men poffeffed of a freehold of the yearly value of ten pounds or

Q   if

if a perfonal eftate I think of three hundred pounds in value, a reftriction which I fincerely wifh was extended to all his Majefty's fubjects in this kingdom without diftinction; and therefore when the noble Lord talks of emancipating the Papifts of Ireland, or of reftoring them to the benefits of the Conftitution he does not fpeak with all the accuracy which might be expected of him; I know of no word more frequently in ufe than the Conftitution, nor of any which is fo often abfent. I will ftate to the noble Lord what my notions are of the Britifh Conftitution; and if I am miftaken he will fet me right. A Government fprings from it which affords equal protection to all his Majefty's fubjects in their characters, their lives, their liberties and their property. Will the noble Lord fay, that the character, the life, the liberty and the property of a Roman Catholic have not the fame protection from the law in this kingdom, that is extended to every other member of the Community.

I take it to be a vital principle of the conftitution, that the church and ftate are intimately and infeperably united, clinging both to the other for fupport; and therefore it is, that every fubject in thefe kingdoms, is bound by laws coeval with the conftitution as now eftablifhed, before he can be admitted to the exercife of any efficient power ecclefiaftical or civil derived under it, to give a folemn and unequivocal pledge of his allegiance to the eftablifhment in Church and State; laws which bind us all indifferently, and therefore, when the

modern

modern cant of Emancipation is applied to the teſt
laws. It ſeems to be a diſtinct avowal by thoſe who
uſe it, that this breach of political Reform means
nothing ſhort of Revolution. The altar is the main
pillar of the throne, and if we ſhall ever be ſo mad
as to repeal the laws made to guard our ecclefiaſtical
eſtabliſhment, we ſhall in my opinion at the ſame
moment ſhake to its foundation the Britiſh monarchy. 'Till the ærea of modern illumination, it
never was ſuppoſed that a limited monarchy could
exiſt without teſt laws ; that they were eſſential to
maintain the conſtitutional balance between the
different powers of which our Government is com-
poſed, to prevent the Crown from committing the
judicial and miniſterial powers of the State to difaffected perſons, and to prevent the people from
committing the great and extenſive powers exerciſed
by their repreſentatives, to perſons of the ſame
deſcription. The founders of the Iriſh Union had
ſagacity to ſee that the firſt neceſſary ſtep in their
plan of Revolution, was to aboliſh all religious
diſtinctions in the State, and it baffles all human
calculation to diſcover any found principle upon
which we have heretofore acted, in outſtripping
them in advances to the attainment of this their
favourite object. When the noble Lord adopts the
modern ſyſtem of Emancipation, I wiſh he would
bring the ſubject forward diſtinctly, and let us view
it in all its bearings : I ſhould thank him to
bring forward a detailed and practicable plan of
rational Government, under his propoſed ſyſtem
of

of emancipation : that he would firſt ſhew us the
practicability of repealing the act of ſupremacy ;
an act which annexes the eccleſiaſtical juriſdiction in
Ireland to the imperial crown of England : I ſhould
thank him to explain how the repeal of this act is
practicable, without the authority of a Britiſh ſtatute, authoriſing the Keeper of the Great Seal in
England to affix it to an act, for making partition
of this juriſdiction in Ireland with his Holineſs the
Pope : and if the two Houſes of Parliament in
Great Britain ſhall paſs ſuch an act, I ſhall thank
the noble Lord for his ſolution of another difficulty,
and that is, in what manner his Majeſty can be enabled to aſſent to an act giving ſuch an authority to
the Keeper of the Great Seal, or to an act repealing
the act of ſupremacy, conſiſtently with the ſtatute
limiting the crown to the Houſe of Hanover, or
with the coronation oath ; and above all, I ſhall
thank the noble Lord, if his plan of emancipation
ſhould take place, to explain his noſtrum for maintaining a Proteſtant Church by a Popiſh State, and
to explain his new ſyſtem of eccleſiaſtical juriſpru-
dence, to be adminiſtered by judges who deny the
ſource of all exiſting eccleſiaſtical authority in theſe
kingdoms. If there ever was a ſubject, which ought
to be treated with an anxious and trembling caution,
it is this ſubject of Catholic claim and demand of
exemption from the teſt laws and act of ſupremacy.
But caution and ſober deliberation have been con-
temptuouſly diſclaimed : the people have been told
from high popular authority, that they ſhould by no
means

means forego the opportunity of the war in urging their claims; that they fhould inftantly embrace, and greatly emancipate; and that they muft extinguifh all members of the community who are ftartled by this magnificent projeƈt, or they will be extinguifhed by them. I might perhaps be excufed for fpeaking with fome degree of warmth on this fubjeƈt, for I was within a hair's breadth of being extinguifhed, immediately after this fublime leffon of great emancipation and general extinguifhment was promulgated.

Upon the fubjeƈt of emancipation, will the noble Lord allow me to make a very earneft requeft to him, and if he will indulge me in it, I fhall really acknowledge myfelf deeply indebted to him: will the noble Lord have the goodnefs on his return to Great Britain, to oblige me, by propofing a repeal of the teft laws and the aƈt of fupremacy, in the Britifh Houfe of Lords? I am pretty confident the noble Lord will not grant me this requeft: and he will not grant it, becaufe he knows, that if he were to make fuch a propofition there, he would foon learn, that it is treafon to the Britifh Conftitution. He would there be taught to know that the Houfe of Stewart was expelled the Britifh throne for a fimilar attempt, and that any man who fhould dare to propofe fuch a repeal in the Britifh Parliament, did by the propofition, condemn the title of the illuftrious houfe of our Monarch to the Britifh throne. If the noble Lord were to talk of repealing the teft laws, and the aƈt of fupremacy in Great Britain, by

way

way of conciliation, he would be told, that he re-
tailed the fulfome cant of James's memorable declaration for liberty of confcience : and I wifh the noble Lord to read that famous proclamation, in which
he will find the ftale and fiimfy pretext of conciliating and uniting men of all religious perfuafions, in
the fupport of Government and the Conftitution,
held out to the people of England by that deluded
bigot, to reconcile them to the introduction of Papifts into both Houfes of Parliament, and into the
efficient offices of the ftate, civil and military.

Upon the fecond head of the noble Lord's conciliatory project, I fhall fay but little : the opinions of
the noble Lord upon this fubject feem to have received a very fudden twift fince his laft arrival in
Ireland. The noble Lord has ftated this night, that
his opinion recently and publicly delivered upon
this fubject, was confined altogether to Parliamentary Reform, in Great Britain ; I muft therefore
conclude, that fuch was the noble Lord's refervation when he delivered that opinion, although it was
delivered without refervation or qualification, in a
debate introduced by him exclufively on the fubject
of Ireland ; but as the noble Lord ftill avows his dif-
approbation of Parliamentary Reform in Great Britain, as a meafure at beft doubtful in point of advantage, and imminently hazardous in the probable
confequences : let me now put it to him, how infinitely more hazardous and critical will be the experiment in this kingdom. If the noble Lord will
look to the political fituation of Great Britain and
Ireland,

Ireland, connected under one common Sovereign, each country governed by a Parliament perfectly diftinct from and independent of the other, the imperial fyftem for both kingdoms, will appear to be the moft critical and complicated that has ever fubfifted in Europe : to a common obferver it would appear to be utterly impracticable : however, experience has proved, that in the midft of popular turbulence, and in the convulfion of rancorous and violent party contefts, the Irifh Parliament as it is now conftituted, is fully competent to all practical and beneficial purpofes of government ; that it is fully competent to protect this, which is the weaker country, againft encroachment, and to fave the empire from diffolution, by maintaining the conftitutional connection of Ireland with the Britifh crown. And, therefore, if the noble Lord feels the imminent hazard of innovation in the conftitution of Great Britain, how much more cautious ought he to be of making experiments in Ireland, more particularly when they have been firft devifed for the avowed purpofe of deftroying the fubtle and attractive principles of adhefion, which have heretofore preferved the empire from diffolution. But let me fuppofe for a moment that the noble Lord's conciliatory fyftem was free from difficulty or objection, will he, as a ftatefman, ferioufly recommend to the Irifh Parliament to yield to rebellion the claimed redrefs of fpeculative political grievances ? Will the noble Lord, as a ftatefman, recommend to us as a meafure of found policy, to repeal our teft laws and act of fupremacy,

premacy, and to reform the other Houfe of Parliament, in the hope by fuch an act of conciliation and
conceffion, to put down a determined rebellion ? If
we are to make fuch a precedent for the encouragement of rebellion, I beg of the noble Lord to fay
where are we to draw the line.; and if he will not
fubfcribe to my opinion on this fubject, I beg to refer him to a Right Hon. Gentleman in another country of the firft ability as a ftatefman, who, in the
year 1783, did moft emphatically declare his opinion as a Cabinet-minifter, that the exiftence of legitimate government in Ireland depended on the difperfion of a military convention, then affembled for
the reform of Parliament, and on the indignant re-
jection of any propofition which they might prefume
to make upon the fubject. In that convention I will
venture to fay there was not a fingle rebel ; there
was not a member of it who would not willingly
have fhed his blood in the defence of his Sovereign
and of the conftitution. But I did then agree with
that Right Hon. Gentleman, that there muft be an
end of all legitimate government, if political claims
are to be advanced at the point of the bayonet ; and
if I did at that period refufe to liften to a propofition
for parliamentary reform, made to the Houfe of
Commons by a military convention, compofed of
very worthy gentlemen, who had been giddily betrayed into fuch an act of indifcretion, I will not
now liften to much more extravagant claims
preffed upon me under the terror of impending rebellion. If the conciliatory fyftem recommended

commended by the noble Lord is to be debated on its intrinfick merits. Let me advife him to apply to the Directory of the Irifh Union in the firft inftance; let the Directory withdraw their minifter plenipoten-tiary from Paris; let them diffolve their revolu-tionary Government at home; let them deliver up their cannon and pikes which have heretofore efcaped the vigilance of civil and military officers; Let them withdraw their emiffaries who have been fent forth to feduce the people from their allegiance, and abfolve them from the treafonable engagements with which they have been feduced; and let them then fubmit their claims and their grievances to calm difcuffion by the Legiflature.

I will once more appeal to the noble Lord, and call upon him to waive all vague and general queftions; and to ftate diftinctly the grievance if it exifts; of which the people of Ireland can with juftice complain againft the Britifh Government, the Britifh Parliament or the Britifh Nation; or againft the Government or Parliament of their own coun-try. In 1779 they demanded a free trade, and it was granted to them. In 1782 they were called upon to ftate the meafure of their grievances, and the redrefs which they demanded; and redrefs was granted to the full extent of their demands. In 1787 they were diffatisfied with the redrefs which they had pointed out, and acknowledged to be complete and fatisfactory, and it was extended to the terms of their new demand. In 1785 they demanded a com-mercial treaty with Great Britain, and fhe made

R   them

them a fair and liberal offer which they were
pleafed to reject with childifh folly. In 1789 they
demanded a place bill, a penfion bill, and a refponfibility bill as neceffary to fecure the Conftitution
eftablifhed in Great Britain and Ireland in 1688,
and renewed in Ireland in 1782, which they pledged
themfelves to fupport to the laft drop of their blood.
They had their place bill, and their penfion bill, and
their refponfibility bill, and much more than they
had ever demanded upon that fcore ; for his Majefty
was pleafed to furrender his hereditary revenue, and
to accept a civil eftablifhment for his life, by which
Parliament was enabled to make a general appropriation of the revenues, and to limit the Crown in
granting penfions ; and his Majefty was alfo pleafed
to put the office of Lord Treafurer into commiffion ;
and by thefe regulations they obtained the fame
fecurity for the Conftitution as eftablifhed at the Revolution in 1688 which the people of Great Britain
enjoy, and at the time when this fecurity was given
to them, the Parliament of Great Britain repealed
and explained the Britifh navigation laws by which
we were prohibited from exporting the produce
of the Britifh colonies and plantations from this
country, to Great Britain, a boon of all others
the moft effential to our foreign trade, for by
it we have the certain iffue of the Britifh market for
any furplus of plantation goods imported into Ireland
above our own confumption. About the fame period every difability which had affected Irifh Papifts
was removed, fave a reftriction in the ufe of fire-
arms,

arms, which extends only to the lowest order of the people ; and sober and thinking men might reasonably have hoped that the stock of grievances was exhausted, and that they might have been allowed some short respite from popular ferment. In this expectation however we have been deceived, and when every other topick of discontent had failed, the government and constitution, as established at the Revolution, has been discovered by the gentlemen who pledged themselves in 1789 to defend and maintain it to the last drop of their blood, to be a slavish monopoly, inconsistent with the civil and religious liberties of the people. And is the noble Lord so credulous in this instance as to suppose that if this new project should succeed, and the slavish monopoly of the Revolution was abolished, the account of grievances would be closed—*Uno avulso non deficit alter, & simili frondescit Virga metallo.*

If the noble Lord wishes to know the genuine source of ostensible Irish grievances, he will be enabled to trace it to some of his political friends and connections in Great Britain and Ireland. The genuine source of Irish complaint against the British government is, that they will not second the ambitious views of some gentlemen who claim an exclusive right to guide the public mind, and to monopolize to themselves and their dependants the power and patronage of the Crown. The genuine cause of complaint against the British Cabinet is, that they will not suffer these gentlemen to erect an aristocratic power in Ireland which shall enable them to dictate

tate

tate to the Crown and the People ; which fhall enable them to direct and controul the adminiftration of
Great Britain, by making the government of this
country impracticable by any but their political
friends and allies. Upon what juft grounds thefe ar-
rogant pretenfions are advanced, I have not as yet
been enabled to difcover. I am willing to give the
noble Lord full credit for the fincerity of his profeffions, and to believe that his object is to tranquillize
this giddy and diftracted country, and therefore I
will take the liberty moft earneftly to advife him
not to renew the ftrange exaggerated ftatements
which he has been in the habit of making on Irifh affairs in the Britifh Houfe of Lords, where they can
have no other effect than mifchief. Let me advife
him alfo moft earneftly to exert the influence which
his high name and character muft give him with his
political connections in Great Britain, to induce
them to confine their political warfare to the theatre of their own country, and to ceafe to dabble in
dirty Irifh faction. It is one great misfortune of this
country that the people of England know lefs of it,
than they know perhaps of any other nation in Europe. Their impreffions I do verily believe to be
received from newfpapers, publifhed for the fole
purpofe of deceiving them. There is not fo vola-
tile nor fo credulous a nation in Europe as the Irifh ;
the people are naturally well difpofed, but are more
open to feduction than any man would credit, who
had not lived amongft them. If I am to fpeak
without difguife, civilization has not made any confiderable

fiderable progrefs amongft us, and therefore the
kingdom of Ireland is, of all the nations of Europe,
the moft dangerous to tamper with, or to make experiments upon. Her prefent difturbed and diftracted ftate has certainly been the confequence of a
feries of experiments practifed upon her for a courfe
of years. If the gentlemen of Ireland who have a
permanent intereft in the fafety of the State, could
be prevailed upon to adjourn their political quarrels
and refentments to a period when they might be renewed, without endangering every thing which is
worth preferving in fociety, and to unite againft the
common enemy, I fhould feel no manner of apprehenfion for the event of the conteft in which we are
engaged, with foreign and domeftic enemies. But
whilft we are divided, and men of rank and character are found ready to hazard every thing for the
poffible fuccefs of little paltry perfonal objects, the
crifis becomes awful indeed. If Ireland is to be
tranquillized, the firft ftep towards it muft be, to
curfh rebellion. No lenity will appeafe the factious
rancour of modern Irifh reformers, nor will any
meafure of conciliation fatisfy them fhort of a pure
democracy, eftablifhed by the influence, and gua-
ranteed by the power of the French Republic.

LORD MOIRA having in his reply ftated, that
he did not wonder the people of Ireland fhould wifh
for Parliamentary Reform, when an official declaration had been made in the Houfe of Commons,
that

that half a million muft be expended to put down
the oppofition. The CHANCELLOR, in anfwer
to this obfervation, thanked his Lordfhip for having
afforded him an opportunity of publickly refuting
a calumny which had been propagated with uncommon induftry. The Chancellor ftated, that in the
feffion of 1789, during the indifpofition of his Majefty, when a debate arofe upon a vote of cenfure
moved againft Lord Buckingham, becaufe he declined to tranfmit an Addrefs to his Royal Highnefs
the Prince of Wales, an obfervation was made in
the Houfe of Commons, by fome other gentleman,
that a cenfure had fome years before been voted
againft Lord Townfhend, and that in the fame Parliament, a flattering Addrefs had been alfo voted to
him. The Chancellor faid, that in adverting to this
obfervation in the courfe of the debate, he ftated
fimply, that he had heard that Addrefs in all its confequences, coft the Irifh nation half a million ; and
the ftory which has been built on this naked obfervation, on a ftatement made in debate by another
gentleman, is, that he had, in defending new offices created by Lord Buckingham, juftified the ex-
penditure of half a million in putting down the oppofition in the Houfe of Commons : he faid he was
not furprifed that Lord Moira had been impofed upon by this impudent falfehood ; but that two plain
facts were fufficient for its detection : one is, that
the new offices complained of, were not created until after he [the Chancellor] had ceafed to be a
member of the Houfe of Commons ; and the fubject

ject never was debated in the Houfe of Lords. The other fact he ftated to be, that when he made the obfervation, he voted in a fmall and virtuous minority in the Houfe of Commons, when fo far from his fpeaking officially, it was generally underftood, that he was to go out of office on the change of Adminiftration, which was expected immediately to take place, fo much fo, that his fucceffor was publickly named. As to the tranfactions in Lord Townfhend's time, he could have fpoken of them merely from report, as at the time they took place, he was at the Univerfity of Oxford.

BISHOP

Bifhop of Down. I hope, my Lords, the very
fevere and perfonal attack which the learned Lord
has made upon me, will juftify me in troubling
your Lordfhips, though unaccuflomed to fpeak
in public.—My Lords, the tone in which the
learned Lord has fpoken of me, renders it impoffible that I fhould not fay fomething to defend
myfelf from an aggreffion fo unprovoked. He
has fpoken of me as if he took it for granted
that neither I nor any of my brethren were juftified in having an opinion of our own on any fubject—as if it were a thing of courfe that we fhould
always adopt the fentiments of Adminiftration,
and that to differ from them in any point were
a flagrant violation of our facred duty. What,
my Lords, have I been charged with? and what
is the crime which has provoked fuch afperity?
I am charged with having been one of many
highly refpectable names who dared to petition
our Common Sovereign, and lay before the father of his people the fufferings under which we
labour. Of the meafure, my Lords, I am proud,
I contend for it, that confidered in a conftitutional point of view it was perfectly legal—and I
am equally convinced that the allegations of it,
notwithftanding what the noble Lord has alledged to the contrary, were perfectly and ftrictly
true. I have not, indeed, compared the formal
and technical returns of the imports and exports
of this or that manufacture for a given year or
two; but I am convinced from ocular and perfonal examination of the general ftate of that part

S   of

of the country, from the general teſtimony of its inhabitants, and from the infallible proof which the aſpect of the country exhibits, that its manufactures and its trade have ſuffered, almoſt to annihilation. The noble and learned Lord, in a tone of confidence which is, ſo peculiar to him, aſſerts that I went about ſoliciting ſignatures to this petition. I aſſert, in oppoſition to the learned Lord, that the information which he has received on that ſubject, is falſe. I deny the fact, but were it true, I ſee nothing in it which either as an honeſt man or a Proteſtant Biſhop, I ſhould be aſhamed of. For this meaſure the learned Lord has endeavoured to hold me forth to this Houſe and the cublic as a pulprit, and when he deſcribes me in that point of view he holds me up emphatically as a BISHOP. Is this the conduct of one profeſſing, as the learned Lord does, ſuch zeal for the ſupport of the eſtabliſhed church? If ſuch be his treatment of his friends, the Catholics have little reaſon to regret his friendſhip.—But what is the impropriety in a Proteſtant Biſhop uniting with his fellow ſubjects in a petition to the Crown? Is the right to petition abrogated, or is it become treaſon to complain? If it be, and that I have tranſgreſſed in this act of mine any law of the land, why have I not been proſecuted? for ſurely the law officers of the Crown did not want inclination for the taſk; or if I had been guilty of any indecorum to the Houſe by exerting what I conſidered a conſtitutional right, why has not the learned Lord come boldly forward to move

move for its cenfure on me. I affure the learned
Lord that to any chaftifement of the Houfe I
fhall fubmit with 'becoming humility, at the
fame time that I fhall entertain for his difappro-
bation or praife the moft perfect indifference. My
Lords, I feel that .I am warm on this fubject—I
pray your Lordfhips pardon, and beg you will
excufe me, if interefted as I muft be in the ftrong
expreffions which have been ufed towards me, I
have not been quite temperate. The Chancellor,
in that ftyle of interrogatory which feems to im-
ply fo much, and which really means fo little,
afks me whether your Lordfhips will meet treafon and murder, and confpiracy, with meafures
of conciliation, with Parliamentary Reform and
Catholic Emancipation! I anfwer, my Lords,
that thefe are the only remedies which in our prefent circumftances are likely to be effectual. Of
Catholic Emancipation, a full and complete
Emancipation, an admiffion to all the rights and
privileges which a fubject can claim, I have been '
always a decided friend ; I have always thought it
was a meafure not merely of found policy, but of
ftrict right; nor has any thing which has fallen
from the noble Lord to-night, or at any former
time, tended in any degree to fhake my confidence in that opinion—equally convinced am I,
that a full and fair Reform of the Reprefentation
of the people is a meafure of wifdom and neceffity—I fee nothing but this meafure which can
now reftore to Ireland the bleffings of tranquillity
and content. I have fome propetry in this coun-

try, it is not a great deal, but it is fufficient to intereft me in the fafety and welfare of the State. I have alfo my preferment in the church, both of thefe bind me to confult the peace and good order of the country; and I declare it to be my firm belief, that unlefs thefe meafures be adopted, my property and that of every other gentleman in the country—nay, the country itfelf is gone! The learned Lord has mentioned fomething of letters which talked of a change of miniftry, I know not whether he alludes to me; if he does, I aver that I have not for many years received any letters from Great Britain which expreffed the moft diftant hope being entertained of a change of minifters. However defireable fuch an event might be to the true friends of both countries, I confefs I fee no reafon to think that that event is not now as diftant as ever. Whatever the fate of the country may be, and I dread that fate—it will be due to the prefent Minifters.

LD. CHANCELLOR When I faw that Rev. Prelate's name figned to a paper, calling a promifcuous meeting of all the inhabitants of the county, to affemble upon an hill near Downpatrick—in a diftrict proclaimed according to law, I believed that fignature to be a grofs impofition on the Public—the Rev. Prelate has avowed it, and I will venture to tell him that it was moft unjuftifiable, illegal and indecent in a proteftant Bifhop of the church of Ireland, to call for a promifcuous meeting, which muft have
amounted

amounted to many thoufands of the infurgents, and I did fay, the requifition was figned by fome of the very magiftrates who had in a memorial to government, averred the county to be in a ftate of difturbance.

LORD DUNSANY fupported the motion ; he faid, that the prefent fyftem was the caufe of the exifting difcontents in a great meafure, and that where the people of Ireland were treated by Government with lenity and indulgence, they were proportionably loyal and grateful. It had been afked of the noble Earl who made the motion, why he had not now brought before the Houfe, a catalogue of thofe enormous cruelties which he had detailed in the Britifh Houfe of Peers? Inftead of being afked fuch a queftion, the noble and learned Lord, fhould rather have thanked him for the conciliating and pacific manner in which he propofed to act.—But if noble Lords wanted fuch a catalogue *he* could furnifh them—he could relate to them not fimply the burning of houfes, but the murder in cool blood of their inhabitants — he could give them an account of three men particularly, who, after having had their houfes burned to the ground, were fhot by the military, whofe prifoners they had for fome time been—and he could add to thefe accounts, numerous inftances of men torn from their family and country, and without the form of a trial tranfported. He declared himfelf a friend to both the meafures of conciliation which had

had been mentioned—Catholic Emancipation, and Parliamentary Reform.

Ld. BLANEY. I fhould not trefpafs one moment on your Lordfhips indulgence, had I not acted in an official fituation in this country ; as fuch I confider myfelf in fome meafure called upon to make a fhort ftatement of affairs, fo far as come within the limits of my experience. I fhall confine myfelf entirely within the circle of my own command, entertaining no doubt but the Noble Earl will confider, that in all fituations of life, effects are proportionate to their caufes : and before we enquire into any act of the Army, or on the part of Adminiftration, we muft inquire into the ftate of the Country previous to the painful neceffity of calling in Military aid. At a period when I received an order to take a command againft the Infurgents in the North, I faw that the caufe between them and the Government was a matter, not involving any topic of what we commonly term Conftitutional, but I found that the rabble had entered the lifts againft the Conftitutional Authority of the Kingdom, to difpute on the very elements of all Government in the abftract. This fury, fubverfive in its object, and deftructive in its means, feemed defirous of bringing back fociety to its original ftate of anarchy ; when the object of a combat is rather a conteft for maftery than the maintenance of legitimate right, I thought, in my humble judgment, that the legal authority of the country, was braved by a vaft banditti, in whofe
                                              myfteries

myfteries and projects embarked the bold, the bad, and the adventurous; in this ftruggle with the State they were affociated, claffed, difci-plined and regimented; and at this period I was called upon to be in 'a fmall degree the minifter of that force, which in times of peril every Go-vernment on the earth, be it whatfoever kind it may, has a right to exert, nay, which it is its bounden duty to exert on behalf of its grand ob-jects, the Peace and Security of Perfons and Pro-perty; the Laws were hufhed, the Juries inti-midated, and Witneffes murdered; yet, in that focus of mifdoing, where it was my fate to ufe the ftronger power which Government muft fometimes ufe for the great object to which I have alluded, I was thought but an auxiliary to the Law; it is true the Law was fo enfeebled as fcarcely to have the appearance of being a prin-cipal; but in that cafe, I muft prefume, when it was enfeebled, it was by being overcome by the enemies of all law and order, the armed Traitors of the Land : the time was exigent and the pe-ril was great; fuch was the fituation of the country when I undertook a command; I was under no obligation to Adminiftration, but acted in obedience to orders, and as the exigen-cies of the times required, in the courfe of that command. Nothing could give me more pleafure than to contradict malicious reports fo induftrioufly circulated, and circulated through a channel I had little reafon to expect, than to meet the ftricteft public inveftigation of

every

every officer and foldier concerned, no complaint
ever having been made by an inhabitant of what
defcription foever that was not immediately en-
quired into by a Court-Martial, and the prifoner, if found guilty, punifhed according to
his fentence; where religious diftinctions prevailed, every idea of that nature was done away,
I knew no party, but every thing yield to military difcipline, and breach of orders alone I
confidered as the greateft crime a foldier could
be guilty of; therefore as commanding officer,
I was in every refpect refponfible for their conduct.—With refpect to the ftate of affairs in
the country, I made all poffible enquiry into ex-
aminations; finding numbers fwearing againft
each other through pique or party prejudice,
I duly weighed the contents of their affidavits, and judged of their veracity; the confequence of which was, I fent but 16 prifoners
to gaol, and out of that number 14 were capitally convicted—I took up numerous concealed
arms and pikes. I never tranfported a man
without trial, and before I left the country
good order was reftored, the laws took their regular courfe, trade and manufactures, fo long at
a ftand, began to flourifh, and the inhabitants,
no longer the fport of defigning men, began to
feel their own confequence, and to enjoy the
pleafures of peace and tranquillity: fuch was the
fituation of the country when I left it—I fhould
be forry to difagree with the noble Earl in any
point; as an officer, I have ferved under him
                                          abroad,

abroad, and no character could have stood in higher estimation than his with the Army; nor can I suppose he could have any idea of throwing blame on an Army, individually; he must know there are articles of war, which if they transgress it is the duty of their superior officers to punish. I presume, my Lords, that in all matters the Government had sufficient intelligence. I am not a sophist, my Lords, I am a plain soldier, and cannot deal in specious or plausible assertion—I am but an adventurous dealer in any profound disquisition—but I take it, that the licenfe which nature has given individuals may well be assumed by Government, which is composed of individuals entrusted with the solemn charge of the security of millions. Government must act on principles of self-defence, when its existence is not only threatened, but its overthrow presumed on as a possibility not resting on speculation—the operation of French principles on the rest of Europe, cannot be light or ineffective, every condition of European society is more or less tainted, and the source of moral happiness more or less impoisoned from that great spring of confusion and anarchy, it behoves Government to make serious enquiry into the state of affairs, this country, my Lords, has had its share of the calamity, for I am not sanguine enough to bespeak an immediate repose to our difficulties. With respect to Parliamentary Reform and Catholic Emancipation, I am sorry they were both blended together, as had Reform alone come forward, it

T   should

ſhould have had my decided ſupport; but both
coming at the ſame time, I think them rather in-
conſiſtent with our preſent ſituation, and therefore oppoſe both.

Lord Viſcount Dillon obſerved, that any
thing falling from the high authority of the noble
Lord, might have a very different effect from
what he might intend. It was moſt probable that
at the very moment in which their Lordſhips
were ſitting in that Houſe, meetings were held
in every part of the kingdom of the diabolical
aſſociation of United Iriſhmen, perhaps at that
very moment debating the inſtant when they
ſhould burſt forth and overturn the country.—
That union of treaſon muſt be met by an union
of courage and loyalty; conciliation was out of
the queſtion. Were we to ſurrender our laws, our
lives, our properties to this fraternity? That was
the kind of conciliation they required, and who
that had a feeling of honour, of loyalty, would
ſubmit to the degradation? It was not eaſy to
conceive how Government could be arraigned
for its conduct; every act of theirs had been
undertaken under the ſanction of Parliament;
the firſt act, the gunpowder bill, had been founded on the report of a Committee of that Houſe;
every other act had been added as the miſchief
ſeemed to increaſe; and his Lordſhip thought
that if more had been done in the beginning,
the neceſſity of ſome of the future proceedings and many thouſands of lives would have
been ſaved. As to the immediate queſtion,
would

would not Government have been liable to be
called to account if they had not exerted their
powers to the prefervation of the country? if
they had not taken from the difaffected the
arms which they would long ago have turned
againft the Conftitution and its fupporters. He
lamented as much as any of their Lordfhips the
incidental mifconduct which had arifen in the
profecution of this laudable purpofe, from the
heated paffions or prejudiced views of the individuals whom it might have been neceffary to en-
truft, and which it was impoffible to prevent.
His Lordfhip concluded by giving his thorough
approbation to Government, for their conduct
in the arduous tafk in which they were at prefent, and had for fome time paft been employed.

The Earl of ORMONDE defended the conduct
of Adminiftration, and faid, that though he was
willing to give the Noble Earl who had brought
forward this meafure this night, credit for the
goodnefs of his intention, yet he could not avoid
faying that he confidered that the propofition
which he had made to the Houfe would, inftead
of conciliating the people, or tranquilizing the
country, tend more to difturb the peace and con-
vulfe the kingdom, than any meafure that could
poffibly have been devifed. The evils that would
refult from the debate of this night, he feared
would produce mifchiefs incalculable, and of
which the Noble Earl did not feem to be aware.
From the moment that the report was circulated
in this country of the Noble Earl's intention to

T 2   come

come to Ireland to agitate the subject, the spirits
and the hopes of the disloyal and discontented
were raised; the outrages in the country had in-
creased, and he was convinced it would require
the utmost vigilance, energy, and exertion of
Government, to guard against the dangers which
presented themselves to his mind, as likely to
flow from the question which the Noble Earl had
brought forward. He knew the purity of his
own intentions, and with this conviction on his
mind, he could not avoid giving his decided ne-
gative to the motion.

The Earl of MOIRA.—My Lords, the noble
Baron who spoke second in this debate, and the
learned Lord on the Woolsack, have both said,
that my arrival in this country has produced
much mischief and greatly inflamed discontent.
If, my Lords, so much danger were to be apprehended by my coming, those whose misre-
presentations so widely and so wantonly circulated of my conduct in another country, made it
necessary that I should come, are chargeable with
the mischief.—The noble Lords have said also,
that the discussion in which we are now engaged
will aggravate the disorders which are already so
mischievous—if so, my Lords, they who have
made the discussion necessary by resisting a motion of conciliation and peace are to be blamed
for the consequences. The noble Baron who
thought fit so eloquently to oppose my motion,
began his speech by insinuating that a something
had taken place somewhere, which with respect

to

to this Houfe he did not think becoming—the
noble Baron appeared to labour under great difficulty in ftating what that fomething was—it
however at laft appeared to be the motion which
I had the honour of fubmitting to the Britifh
Parliament on this fubject. But the noble Baron,
though apparently much difcontented with my
fpeech on that occafion, could not ftate exactly
in what the irregularity of it confifted. The
learned Lord on the Woolfack, who followed
him, declared himfelf equally diffatisfied with my
conduct on that occafion, but laboured under the
fame difficulty in ftating what the breach of order or want of refpect to this Houfe confifted.
Of my attachment to the independence of the
Irifh Legiflature, neither of the noble Lords furely can entertain any doubt—and it behoved the
learned Lord, who feems alfo to charge my conduct on that occafion with being hoftile to that
independence, to have known that the motion
which I then made, was perfectly confiftent with
the perfect independence of the Legiflature of
Ireland, and confonant to that fpirit on which
the connexion of the two countries is founded.
The learned Lord fhould have known that the
Lord Lieutenant of this country is appointed by
a commiffion under the Great Seal of England—
that he receives his inftructions from the Secretary of State, and under the King's Signet—that
he is bound to obey the inftructions which he
receives through the medium of that Secretary,
a Member of the Britifh Cabinet, and that therefore

fore it is under the fpecial inftruction of that
Cabinet that he acts. Through what channel
then could application be made to correct the
abufes of the Irifh Executive, but through the
channel of the Britifh Parliament, to whom only
that Cabinet is refponfible ? The learned Lord
might have learned further on the fubject—he
might have learned that if the conduct of an
Irifh Lord Lieutenant, is not cenfurable by the
Britifh Legiflature, the Irifh Lord Lieutenant,
holds a fituation which the Britifh Conftitution
difclaims and abhors—a fituation deftitute of refponfibility, for the Irifh Parliament cannot take
cognizance of the conduct of the Viceroy appointed by the Crown and Cabinet of Great
Britain. The jurifdiction of the Britifh Parliament, over the conduct of the Irifh Viceroy, the
learned Lord might have feen afcertained by the
higheft authority, by Lord Coke himfelf, who
lays it down as a principle, that wherever the
King's feals go, there does the authority of Parliament extend. But laying afide thefe arguments, which from the nature of them the noble
Lord might be fuppofed to know, there is another which proved that in what I did on that occafion I was perfectly well founded—it was that
though the fubject of my motion was far from
agreeable to the majority of the Britifh Peers, yet
no attempt was made to flop me from proceeding under any fuppofed idea that the fubject was
one unfit for the difcuffion of that Houfe. A
great number of the Britifh Peers were by no

means

means politically friends to me—they would, therefore have gladly availed themfelves of fuch an objection to the motion had it been liable to fuch objection. The learned Lord in a very long fpeech has gone into an elaborate, and I will al-low, an able detail of the conceffions which Great Britain has made to Ireland, for fome years back. I do not fee how that detail bears on the prefent queftion, but I will fay, of thofe fucceffive de-mands and conceffions which have been made, that they were fuch as in an improving country, might naturally have been expected. Every new advantage which Ireland enjoyed enlarged her fphere of action, and made her know the value of, and feel the neceffity for others. I will fay ftill farther, that if thefe were conceffions made to the demands of Ireland, they were equally be-neficial to Great Britain, for the wealth of Ire-land is the ftrength of Great Britain, as I would fay that the weaknefs or poverty of Great Bri-tain would be the calamity of Ireland.

The learned Lord afks me whether I do not believe that there exifts in this country a dangerous confpiracy againft the Government? My Lords, I do believe there exifts fuch a con-fpiracy, and I attribute the exiftence of that confpiracy to the fevere meafures which Go-vernment have adopted; I attribute much of the danger and much of the difturbances which exift, to that moft impolitic and lamentable meafure—the recall of my Lord Fitzwilliam; I predicted it when I firft heard of that mea-

fure,

fure, and I have been too true a prophet.
The fyftem which was continued fubfequent to
that event, a fyftem of coercion, of cruelty, and
of blood, has aggravated the evil, and driven the
people to the moft dangerous and unconftitution-
al fteps, as means of fuppofed felf-defence againft
the extreme feverity of their Government. The
learned Lord had thought proper to allude to
newfpapers and pamphlets, and argue from what
they report as my fpeech, as if it were really
mine. In one of thófe publications, I am made
to fay what certainly I never faid, that the troops
in Ireland were taught to look on every Irifhman
as a rebel, and treat him accordingly. It would
have been extremely abfurd in me to have ufed
fuch an expreffion, generally, of the troops in
Ireland, for many of thofe troops are themfelves
Irifh. What I faid was, " that the foreign troops
which were fent to Ireland went thither under
an unfortunate prejudice, which care had been
taken to inftil into them, that every man they
met there was a rebel." His lordfhip is alfo
pleafed to fay, that he would not, were he a general officer, commanding the army in Ulfter,
be much obliged to me for faying that I was fure
they did not act with their inclination in difcharging the late orders of Government. I am
fure that thefe officers would find it an unpleafant
duty, were they bound to execute on the people
a punifhment legally inflicted. I am fure it muft
be ftill more fo, where they are obliged to exert
meafures of extraordinary feverity. I know too
the

the delicate fituation in which an officer is placed, when he is appointed to execute fuch orders as thofe under which General Leake and others acted. I know how difficult it is in fuch circum-ftances to avoid being mifled by the miftate-ments, the falfehood or the paffions of others, to acts perhaps more fevere than the truth of circumftances would warrant. With refpect to the crimes which had been perpetrated in the county of Armagh, I did ftate in that fpeech that I believed the Government might have con-nived at the enormities which were there prac-tifed, and certainly thofe enormities committed againft a clafs of men at that time known to be fufpected by Government as hoftile, and com-mitted by the palpable connivance of the magif-trates might well juftify the fufpicion. Another of the meafures which, taking my fpeech from the public prints, his Lordfhip afferts, I attribu-ted to Government, without any rational ground, was the publication of the *Union Star.* Without enquiring very minutely what thofe publications may have faid of me, I will tell the learned Lord what I did fay on that occafion : I did fay that, there was fomething fo extrava-gantly abfurd in that paper, fomething fo incon-fiftent with its profeffed end, affaffination, in defcribing publicly the names of the perfons to be affaffinated, who would naturally be put upon their guard, that I did think, and I ftill retain that opinion, that it was as likely to be written by the enemies of that party on whom

U   the

the imputation of it was to fall, as by the party itſelf.

But of the faɛs which I allude to in the Britiſh Houſe of Peers, as proofs of the extreme cruelty of the ſyſtem which was carried on in Ireland, his Lordſhip denies the truth. One of thoſe faɛs was the ſtrangling of one Shaw, in order to in-duce a confeſſion, and his Lordſhip aſſerts that the rope *was only put round his neck*, but that he was not actually ſuſpended. I repeat my former aſ-ſertion, that he did actually undergo a proceſs of ſtrangulation, and that more than once. His Lordſhip has alluded to another part of my ſpeech, and triumphantly denies that the curfew regulation was of rigorouſly enforced in a parti-cular inſtance as I was ſuppoſed to have mention-ed. In deſcribing the ſeverity of ſo arbitrary a meaſure, I took the liberty to ſuppoſe a caſe in which the enforcement of it would be attended with great hardſhip, the caſe was that of a pa-rent watching at night over his dying child, and obliged in ſuch circumſtances to put out his lights by the order of a military patrol. It ſo happen-ed that ſuch a caſe as this did occur though with ſome circumſtances leſs aggravating than I had ſtated. The papers related this ſuppoſition of mine as if it had been a real faɛt I had been deſ-cribing, and his Lordſhip ſuppoſing me convict-ed of error in this inſtance, labours to prove that therefore the other faɛs which I had related de-ſerved no credit.—But to paſs over theſe leſs im-portant points and come to the buſineſs before us. The learned Lord aſks whether I would oppoſe the ſlow proceſs of laws to men banded

in

in open rebellion? I will anfwer the queftion by bidding him fhew me the rebellion, and while I afk him to do fo, I cannot help ex-preffing my regret that his Lordfhip deals fuch ftrong charges fo liberally, and flings the epi-thet REBEL on the whole kingdom of Ireland. My Lords, before a nation be convicted of this heavy crime, and the punifhment of it inflicted, there ought to be fome proof—there ought to be the ftrongeft proofs.—Where are they?—The learned Lord has brought the cafe of Col. Haynes to juftify the fyftem which has been carried on in Ireland.---Let me ftate to your Lordfhips what that cafe was:—Ifaac Haynes had been taken at the capture of Charleftown—He was fuffered to go on parole to his own houfe—He was not content-ed with remaining a prifoner on parole—he vo-luntarily came forward and took the oath of alle-giance – he foon began to intrigue, and obtained the command of Colonel of Militia in the enemy's army—he corrupted a battalion of our Militia which had been enrolled and attefted—he was de-tected carrying them off at the very moment when the enemy were coming down upon us. He was identified before a court of enquiry and exe-cuted. But it is neceffary to inform your Lordfhips that this court of enquiry was almoft the only cri-minal court known in the country, the diftance from head quarters impeding the poffibility of procuring from the commander and chief a war-rant to hold a court martial, it was adopted from the example of the enemy, and it was fo far fuperior to a court martial that the officer who

U 2　　　　　　　　prefided

prefided in it was refponfible for every officia
act. But what analogy would the learned
Lord draw between this cafe and any which
can occur in Ireland? America was in a ftate of
open rebellion—there was of courfe a complete
diffolution of civil government. Does the noble Lord mean to fay that fuch is the ftate of
Ireland? He ought to know that in Ireland in its
prefent circumftances, martial law cannot exift in
any part of it. Would he make the exiftence of
a Society of United Irifhmen, however culpable
or mifled they may be, a pretext for the fufpen-
fion of civil government, and for laying the country proftrate under a military force? Tyranny
only could reafon thus—Tyranny which never
wants a colour to give a fhade to its true defigns.
America was then in a ftate of rebellion. Ireland
is ftill at peace, and yet I will venture to fay,
that there were fewer capital and fummary executions in America for twelve months of that
period, than there have been in Ireland for the
laft year!

But the noble Baron near me has read to the
Houfe a fhocking catalogue of the murders which
have been perpetrated by the infurgents—he has
mentioned among them the recent one of a generous and valiant officer—it is horrid indeed in all
its circumftances, and I feel its full horror—But
do thefe dreadful crimes furnifh any argument on
this queftion? If they do, I will find for the noble
Baron another crime to match it, equally horrid
—If he go on with his reckoning, I will accompany

pany him and find him death for death. But
furely, we are not here to fettle an account of
blood. I wifhed to avoid the fhocking recital,
and hoped that at laft a meafure of conciliation and peace would have been received. I have
been afked, why I did not here bring forward
that lift of cruelties and murders which I had mentioned in the other Houfe of Peers. It was for
this reafon—becaufe I thought it would have
been for the benefit, for the honour of the country, if all that had paffed had been forgotten.
But let it not be fuppofed, that the enormitie*
which have been committed in this country are
for ever buried in oblivion. If your Lordfhips
fhall not agree to this motion, I fhall immediately move for a Committee to enquire into thefe
crimes, and by what means they have been perpetrated and remain unpunifhed—If they are not
denied I will take them as admitted and lamented, for I fincerely hope they are fo. But if they
are denied, I will bring fuch proof to your bar
as will extort belief, and the proceedings of the
Committee on that fubject fhall convey the grievances and fufferings of the Irifh people to the
Throne.

The noble Lord afks whether I believe Reform
and Emancipation will conciliate? I think they
will. They will give to the people of this country every thing they can want—nor can I believe
that after what has been done by France in every
nation in which fhe has had interference, there
are many people in Ireland fo mad as to wifh to
fee

fee a French army in this country. The people of
Ireland are not fo dull. If any entertain a wifh fo
abfurd, it muft be fuggefted by the delirium to
which men are driven by the fevere and unre-
lenting meafures with which Government have
purfued them. If that fyftem be relaxed, and in
the place of cruel and harfh meafures, mild and
conciliatory meafures are adopted, the people will
ceafe to be deluded. Grant them thefe two great
objects of their purfuit, and even though attempts
fhould ftill be made to miflead them, the means
of doing fo will be removed. But while pains
and penalties are fixed at every corner of their
path, can it be expected they fhall walk in them
with pleafure and contentment ?

But his Lordfhip afks you can you believe that
thefe men mean really nothing more than Reform
and Emancipation ? I afk what reafon has the
Houfe to believe they have any other ultimate
and remote object ? The proof his Lordfhip gives
you is a letter of Mr. Tone's, in which he declares,
when he is forming a conftitution for the United
Irifhmen, that it is his private opinion, that all
they are doing will be of little ufe, and that nothing fhort of a feparation will be effectual. To
this I anfwer, that it is apparent from the words
of this letter itfelf, that Mr. Tone did not believe
that his opinion was that of the perfons to whom
he addreffes himfelf, nor can I think it reafonable to fuppofe when men profefs to look for objects that are certainly ufeful to them that it is
not thefe but others that they aim at.—Now can
any

any man doubt whether the events that have taken place in Ireland for fome years back gave
both to Catholic and the Prefbyterian an intereft
in both of thefe meafures? The Prefbyterian
when he heard it declared in Parliament itfelf
that fuch was its conftitution, that half a million
had been expended to pacify one oppofition, and
that another half million would be wanted for the
fame purpofe? Would he not naturally conceive
himfelf interefted in obtaining a more œconomical
Reprefentation of the People? and would it not
be natural for the Catholic to fuppofe that if any
perfons of his perfuafion were in the Reprefentative body, fo many hundred Catholic families
would not have been driven from their homes and
country without meeting any redrefs from the
Magiftrate or the Legiflature?—The learned Lord
afked whether I have confidered how far Catholic Emancipation was practicable confiftently with
the Conftitution?—I anfwer that I have—Catholic Emancipation is an ill chofen phrafe ufed at
prefent to fignify the admiffion of the Catholic
to a participation of the powers of the State. At
prefent there is nothing which prevents a Catholic Peer from taking his feat in this Houfe, but
the oath of fupremacy—there is no principle of
the Conftitution which forbids it, and it deferves
well to be confidered whether the fpeculative religious opinions of a man fhould prevent this en-
joyment of his civil rights—nothing more fhould
be required on that head than fuch a fecurity from
a man as would prevent him from ufing the
power

power with which he is entrusted to effect a subversion of the Constitution or Religion of the
state.—As to those statements of the trade of Belfast which I had mentioned in my speech on this
sub-ject in Great Britain, and which the learned
Lord has contradicted—I certainly did not take
that statement from the Custom-house returns; my
information on the subject I derived partly from
the commuuication of merchants whom I occafi-
onally faw from that port, and who in thofe communications I have full certainty did not mean to
deceive me.—It was a fubject however in which
error might take place—but I formed my opinion on the fubject from fomething more certain
than thofe loofe communications.—I formed it
from the great diminution which had taken place
in the American trade of that port—In the year
between January 1795 and 1796 there failed
twenty five fhips from the port of Belfaft—in the
year ending January 1797, there were but *twelve*,
and in the year ending January 1798, there was
but *one !*

The learned Lord has chought fit when fpeaking of the U. Irifhmen, their Executive Directory, and their ambaffadors, to fay that his Lordfhip
thought I was not unacquainted with them.—
I know not exactly whether he means by this,
[The Chan. interrupted to explain, he only meant
that as the ambaffadors at Lifle were certainly
Belfaft men, the noble Earl probably might have
known them, though certainly not in their diplo-
matic capacity—] I do think it is fometimes not
                                                    very

very difficult to know the perfons who tranfact the bufinefs of that fociety, for if I am rightly informed, Adminiftration themfelves have been confulting with one of thofe gentlemen, Mr. Neilfon, about what terms would fatisfy the people. I do certainly not difapprove of the meafure, I think every meafure which tends to conciliation and a final adjuftment with the difcontented of the country is ufeful, I only think it proves that Government, though they have confined this very man for feveral months, fo long indeed that I hear he will lofe the ufe of fome of his limbs, are now beginning to entertain lefs ftrong fufpicions of his guilt. His Lordfhip concluded by recapitulating thofe of his arguments which urged the neceffity of Catholic Emancipation and Reform ; the fituation of this country was not an ordinary fituation, and therefore called for no ordinary meafures. Thefe meafures were of fuch a kind that if not fuccefsful they would not at leaft injure, they would leave us where we were, which no doubt, was a fituation fufficiently difaftrous ; and even in the worft event would give to the Houfe and the Government the confolation to reflect that they had done every thing which wifdom and duty had fuggefted to fave the country.

Lord Rosmore, after paying fme handfome compliments to Lord Camden, obferved, that the fair point of view in which to confider the army, was to recollect its conduct before the violent outrages were committed, which now difgrace

X   this

this country ; and from the knowledge he had of
the army, when he had the honour to command
it, he could venture to affirm that there was not
a more conftitutional army, or one more amenable to the laws of the land. Having during that
period frequent communication with Earl Camden, he could fay, that his manners, his principles, and his conduct were of a nature fo conciliatory, that if it had been poffible for any individual to have quieted the country, his Excellency
would have done it ; but Lord Rofmore thought
this country in a ftate of fmothered rebellion,
and that Lord Camden did not apply coercion
early enough.

He had long known the Earl of Moira, and had
the higheft refpect for him, but he could
not praife where he did not approve ; he was
forry for the part he had taken, and feared the
hopes given to the difaffected by his Lordfhip's
fpeeches in England and in Ireland, would do
much more mifchief than the adoption of his
meafures would do good.

The Earl of Bellamont, obferved, that if it was
fuppofed by the noble Earl, that this motion went
to pledge the Houfe to Reform and Emancipation,
he could not vote for it, as he was by no means,
difpofed towards thefe meafures, and as he did
not wifh to vote againft the noble Earl, he would
withdraw during the divifion.

The Earl of Moira faid, the motion went only
in general terms, to approve of conciliation, and
pledged the Houfe to no particular meafure.

At

At half paft two in the morning, the Houfe divided :

Contents,   -   -   -   9
Proxy,   -   -   -   1
Teller, Earl of Moira,   -   -   —10
Not-Contents,   -   -   44
Proxy,   -   -   -   1
Teller, Lord Glentworth,   -   —45

Majority againft the Motion,   -   35

The names of the minority are as follow :—

Earls Charlemont,	Earl Moira,
—— Bellamont,	Lord Dunfany,
—— Arran,	—— Cloncurry,
—— Kilkenny,	and
—— Granard,	The Bifhop of Down.
—— Belvedere,	*Proxy*, Earl Mt. Cafhel.

After the divifion, the following proteft was entered :

Diffentient.

Becaufe that, at a moment when Government has thought itfelf obliged to exert unufual rigour, it appears the extreme of impolicy not to profefs the reluctance with which fuch feverities are enforced, and the wifh of Government to conciliate the minds of the people by a gentler courfe.

Granard,	Wm. Down and Connor,
Moira,	Dunfany,
Charlemont,	Mount Cafhel, (by
Arran,	Proxy.)

APPENDIX.

APPENDIX,

Containing Original Papers, referred to in the foregoing Speeches.

Die Jovis, 7° Martii, 1793.°

The Lord Chancellor from the Lords' Committee appointed to enquire into the caufes of the diforders and difturbances which prevail in feveral parts of this kingdom, to endeavour to difcover the promoters of them, to prevent their extenfion, and to report the refult of their enquiries to the Houfe, made the following Report, *viz.*

My Lords,

THE Committee appointed to enquire into the caufes of the diforders and difturbances which prevail in feveral parts of this kingdom, to endeavour to difcover the promoters of them, to prevent their extenfion, and to report the refult of their enquiries, to the Houfe, have examined into the matters to them referred as far as the time would permit, but apprehending that delay may be attended with danger in the prefent circumftances of the times, they think it their duty to lay before the Houfe immediately fuch information as they conceive to be material for the prefent, which is as follows :

The people at this time called Defenders, are very different from thofe who originally affumed that appellation, and are all, as far as the Committee could difcover, of the Roman Catholic perfuafion ; in general poor ignorant labouring men, fworn to fecrecy, and impreffed with an opinion that they are affifting the Catholic caufe ; in other refpects they do not appear to have any diftinct particular object in view, but they talk of being relieved from hearth-money, tithes, county ceffes, and of lowering their rents. They firft appeared in the county of *Louth*, in confiderable bodies in *April* laft, feveral of them were armed, they affembled
moftly

moftly in the night, and forced into the houfes of Proteftants, and took from them their arms. The diforders foon
fpread through the counties of *Meath, Cavan, Monaghan,*
and other parts adjacent ; at firft they took nothing but
arms, but afterwards they plundered the houfes of every
thing they could find. Their meafures appear to have been
concerted.and conducted with the utmoft fecrecy, and a degree of regularity and fyftem, not ufual in people in fuch
mean condition, and as if directed by men of a fuperior
rank. Sums of money to a confiderable amount, have been
levied and ftill continue to be levied upon the Roman Catholics in all parts of the kingdom, by fubfcriptions and col-
lections at their Chapels and elfewhere ; fome of which levies have been made, and ftill continue to be made under the
authority of a printed circular letter which has been fent
into all parts of the kingdom ; a copy of which letter we
think it our duty to infert herein.

" Sir,

" By an order of the Sub-Committee, dated the fifteenth
" of *January,* I had the honour to forward you a plan for
" a general fubfcription, which had for its object the raifing
" a fund for defraying the heavy and growing expences in-
" curred by the General Committee, in conducting the
" affairs of the Catholics of *Ireland* ; as feveral miftakes
" have occurred in the tranfmiffion of thefe letters, owing
" to my ignorance of the addrefs of many of the delegates,
" I am directed to inform you, that fuch a plan is now in
" forwardnefs throughout the kingdom. A meafure fo
" ftrongly enforced by neceffity, and fo confonant to juf-
" tice, cannot fail to attract your very ferious attention,
" the Committee having the moft perfect reliance on your
" zeal, are therefore confident that you will ufe your beft
" exertions to carry this neceffary bufinefs into full effect.

" *Dublin. February* 5th, 1793.
Signed by the
Secretary of the Sub-Committee.

" P. S. It is hoped that you will acknowledge the re-
" ceipt of this letter, ftating at the fame time whatever
" progrefs has been made in your diftrict."

Several feditious and inflammatory papers publifhed in
Dublin, and difperfed through the country, feem to have
countenanced and encouraged the Defenders in their proceedings ;

ceedings ; and it appears that letters were written by a member of the committee of the Roman Catholics at *Dublin*, previous to the laſt Summer aſſizes, to a perſon reſident at *Dundalk*, in one of which the ſaid perſon in the name of the ſaid Roman Catholic Committee, directed enquiries to be made, touching the offences of which the Defenders then in confinement were accuſed, which enquiries will be beſt explained by inſerting the ſaid letter in the words following.

Dublin, 9th *Auguſt*, 1792.

" Dear Sir,

" I received this day your favour of the 8th inſtant, en-
" cloſing the different papers reſpecting the buſineſs I wrote
" you. It is with much regret that I am obliged to reply,
" that from the want of information on the ſubject matter
" of the indictments, no precife opinion can be formed
" whether the alledged offence is or is not bailable ; the
" Committee are conſequently in the dark as to the mea-
" ſures that ſhould be adopted, nor can your exertions ac-
" celerate (as it feems) that period until the aſſizes, when
" you will be able to obtain office copies of the examina-
" tions. Mr. *Nugent*'s brother left town this day truly
" diſconſolate, in not being able to effect ſomething towards
" the liberation of his kinſman, he however did his beſt in
" the affair.

" I am, dear Sir,
" Your obedient Servant,
" *John Sweetman.*"

" P. S. If any new occurrence ſhould happen, be good
" enough to inform me of it."

And it does appear that the ſaid perſon to whom the ſaid letter was addreſſed at *Dundalk*, did employ at a conſiderable expence, an agent and counſel to act for ſeveral perſons who were accuſed of being Defenders, and were indicted for offences committed by them in the county of *Louth* ; one of which offenders appears to be particularly named in the above letter. But the committee think it their duty to ſtate, that nothing appeared before them which could lead them to believe, that the body of the Roman Catholics in this kingdom were concerned in promoting or countenancing ſuch diſturbances, or that they were privy to this application of any part of the money which had been levied upon them ; however ſuſpicious the conduct of ill-diſpoſed indi-

viduals

viduals of their perfuafions, refident in *Dublin*, may have been. If all the magiftrates in the difturbed counties had followed the fpirited example of the few, who, much to their honour, exerted themfelves with vigour and courage to fupport the laws ; the committee are perfuaded that thefe difturbances might have been fuppreffed: but inftead of doing fo, much the greater part of them remained inactive. The committee are of opinion that the beft means of reftoring permanent tranquillity in the difturbed counties, would be to procure a fufficient number of active, refolute and fteady magiftrates therein, who would exert themfelves to maintain the public peace, and to cut off from thefe deluded people, all hope or expectation of fupport or defence, arifing from a common fund to be levied upon perfons of their communion.

An unufual ferment has for fome months paft difturbed feveral parts of the north, particularly the town of *Belfaft* and the county of *Antrim;* it is kept up and encouraged by feditious papers and pamphlets of the moft dangerous tendency, printed at very cheap and inconfiderable rates in *Dublin* and *Belfaft*, which iffue almoft daily from certain focieties of men or clubs, in both thofe places, calling themfelves committees under various defcriptions, and carrying on a conftant correfpondence with each other. Thefe publications are circulated amongft the people with the utmoft induftry, and appear to be calculated to defame the Government and Parliament, and to render the people diffatisfied with their condition and with the laws. The conduct of the French is fhamefully extolled, and recommended to the public view as an example for imitation ; hopes and expectations have been held up of their affiftance by a defcent upon this kingdom ; and prayers have been offered up at *Belfaft* from the pulpit, for the fuccefs of their arms, in the prefence of military affociations which have been newly levied and arrayed in that town. A body of men affociated themfelves in *Dublin* under the title of the firft national battalion, their uniform copied from the French, green turned up with white, white waiftcoat and ftriped trowfers, gilt buttons impreffed with a harp and letters importing " Firft National Battalion," no Crown, but a device over the harp, of a cap of Liberty upon a pike ; two pattern coats were left at two fhops in Dublin. Several bodies of men have been collected in different parts of the North, armed and difciplined under officers chofen by themfelves, and

compofed

compofed moftly of the loweft claffes of the people. Thefe
bodies are daily encreafing in numbers and force; they have
exerted their beft endeavours to procure military men of experience to act as their officers; fome of them having ex-
prefsly ftated that there were men enough to be had, but
that officers were what they wanted. Stands of arms and
gunpowder to a very large amount, much above the common confumption, have been fent within thefe few months
paft to Belfaft and Newry; and orders given for a much
greater quantity, which it appears could be wanted only for
military operations. At Belfaft, bodies of men in arms are
drilled and exercifed for feveral hours almoft every night by
candle-light, and attempts have been made to feduce the
foldiery, which, much to the honour of the King's forces,
have proved ineffectual. The declared object of thefe military bodies is to procure a reform of Parliament, but the
obvious intention of moft of them appears to be to overawe
the Parliament and the Government, and to dictate to both.
The Committee forbear mentioning the names of feveral
perfons, left it fhould in any manner affect any criminal
profecution, or involve the perfonal fafety of any man who
has come forward to give them information. The refult
of their inquiries, is, that in their opinion it is incompatible
with the public fafety and tranquillity of this kingdom, to
permit bodies of men in arms to affemble when they pleafe,
without any legal authority; and that the exiftence of a
felf-created reprefentative body of any defcription of the
King's fubjects, taking upon itfelf the government of them,
and levying taxes or fubfcriptions, to be applied at the difcretion of fuch reprefentative body, or of perfons deputed
by them, is alfo incompatible with the public fafety and
tranquillity.

To which the Houfe agreed.

Dublin Caftle, 3d *March*, 1797.

SIR,

I am commanded by my Lord Lieutenant to acquaint
you, that from the information received by his Excellency
with refpect to various parts of the North of Ireland, addi-
tional meafures to thofe hitherto employed for preferving
the public peace, are become neceffary. It appears that in
th-

the counties of Down, Antrim, Tyrone, Derry and Done-
gal, secret and treasonable associations still continue to an
alarming degree, and that the persons concerned in these
associations are attempting to defeat all the exertions of the
loyal and well disposed, by the means of terror; that they
threaten the lives of all who shall venture, from regard to
their duty and oath of allegiance, to discover their treasons;
that they assemble in great numbers by night, and by threats
and force disarm the peaceable inhabitants; that they have
fired on his Majesty's justices of the peace when endeavouring to apprehend them in their nocturnal robberies; that
they threaten by papers, letters, and notices, the persons
of those who shall in any manner resist or oppose them;
that in their nightly excursions for the purpose of disarming
his Majesty's loyal subjects, they disguise their persons and
countenances; that they endeavour to collect great quantities of arms in concealed hiding places; that they have cut
down great numbers of trees on the estates of the gentry,
for the purpose of making pikes; that they have stolen great
quantities of lead for the purpose of casting bullets; that
they privately by night exercise themselves in the practice of
arms; that they endeavour to intimidate persons from join-
ing the yeomanry corps established by law in order to resist
a foreign enemy; that they refuse to employ in manufactures those who enlist in the said corps; that they not
only threaten but ill treat the persons of the yeomanry, and
even attack their houses by night, and proceed to the barbarous extremity of deliberate and shocking murder, as was
exemplified in their recent attack, and murder by night, of
Mr. Comyns of Newtown Ards, and that they profess a re-
solution to assist the enemies of his Majesty, if they should
be enabled to land in this kingdom.

It further appears, that these disturbances and outrages
exist and even increase, as well in the districts which have
been proclaimed, as in other parts of the country.

In order therefore to reduce the persons engaged in the
aforesaid treasonable associations, and guilty of the said atro-
cious outrages, to subordination to the laws, and to give
confidence to the well disposed among his Majesty's subjects,
and security to their properties and their lives, and to prevent any assistance being given to the enemy by the disloyal
and disaffected; his Excellency has commanded me to communicate to you his positive orders, that you take the most
immediate and decisive measures for disposing of the mili-

Y   tary

tary force under your command, aided by the yeomanry corps, for immediately difarming all perfons who fhall not bear his Majefty's commiffion, or are acting under perfons fo commiffioned, or perfons holding commiffions under the authority of the yeomanry act, or perfons acting under officers fo commiffioned, and after making fuch difpofition, you are required to carry fuch difarming into effect.

His Excellency gives you this full authority, in order to give your difcretion the greateft latitude, relying at the fame time on your prudence and difcernment in the exercife of it, fo that the peaceable and well affected may be protected againft the evil defigns of thofe who have threatened their lives and property with deftruction.

His Excellency further authorizes you to employ force againft any perfons affembled in arms, not legally authorized fo to be, to difperfe all tumultuous affemblies of perfons, though they may not be in arms, without waiting for the fanction and affiftance of the civil authority, if in your opinion the peace of the realm or the fafety of his Majefty's faithful fubjects may be endangered by waiting for fuch authority.

His Excellency further authorizes you to confider thofe parts of the country where the outrages before ftated have been committed, or where they fhall arife, as being in a ftate that requires all the meafures of exertion and precaution which a country depending upon military force alone for its protection would require; and you are therefore required, to ftation your troops with a view to interrupt communication between thofe whom you may have reafon to fufpect of evil defigns; to eftablifh patroles on the high roads or other paffes, and to ftop all perfons paffing and repaffing after certain hours of the night; and in order completely to carry into effect any orders or regulations, which in the circumftances of the cafe may be confidered by you as neceffary, you are authorized to iffue notices ftating the regulations, and calling upon his Majefty's fubjects to be aiding and affifting therein.

I have the honour to be, &c.

To Lieut. Gen. Leake. T. P.

Dublin,

Dublin Castle, 18th May, 1797.

MY LORD,

The Lord Lieutenant and Council having judged it expedient to call upon his Majesty's troops to exert their utmost force to suppress a seditious and traiterous conspiracy of persons stiling themselves United Irishmen, I am commanded by his Excellency to transmit to your Lordship a copy of the proclamation issued on this subject, and to desire that your Lordship will issue the necessary orders to the troops under your command in consequence thereof. His Excellency has directed me to represent to your Lordship, that as the traiterous and treasonable designs of these conspirators extend to the subversion of the constitution and government, it will be necessary to take measures of general precaution, so that the troops may be prepared to act, whenever it becomes necessary to have recourse to their exertions. In those parts of the kingdom where these designs have been manifested by acts of open violence, it will be necessary to give the officers of his Majesty's troops more precise directions for their conduct. In such parts of the kingdom as have been disturbed by nocturnal depredations, where the lives of his Majesty's loyal subjects have been endangered by persons collected in arms, attacking and firing upon their houses, and where assemblies of persons have been collected for the purpose of unlawfully cutting down trees, or perpetrating other acts of outrage, military precaution should be adopted for the security of the lives and property of his Majesty's loyal subjects, and opposing by the most effectual means such daring acts of violence.

Diligent enquiry should be made respecting any concealed arms or ammunition, and for pikes, and pike handles, and upon information thereof, officers commanding parties should be directed to search for and seize the same.

Any persons armed with pikes or other weapons, in resistance of his Majesty's troops, are to be considered as rebels and treated accordingly. All persons exercising themselves in the use of arms, under persons not holding his Majesty or the Lord Lieutenant's commission, are to be disarmed and apprehended, and in case of resistance to be treated as rebels, and as it appears to be a part of the system of these conspirators to take the opportunity of funerals and other occasions to assemble considerable numbers of persons, the officers of his Majesty's army should be directed in pursuance

ance of this proclamation, to watch all fuch affemblies, and if from their number or other circumftances the public peace fhould appear to be endangered, they will difperfe them ; and as various attempts have been made to feduce his Majefty's troops from their duty and allegiance, you will direct all perfons of fufpicious appearance, who fhall come within the lines of any encampment, barrack, or other ftations of his Majefty's troops, to be detained.

And his Excellency further defires that your Lordfhip will, from time to time, communicate fuch inftructions to the officers of his Majefty's troops, as you fhall deem beft adapted, for carrying into effect his Excellency's proclamation, and as local exigencies may demand.

I have the honour to be,

My Lord,

Your Lordfhip's moft obedient,

Humble fervant,

To Earl Carhampton, THOMAS PELHAM.
Commander in Chief.

In obedience to the order of the Lord Lieutenant in Council, it is the Commander in Chief's commands, that the military do act without waiting for directions from the civil magiftrates, in difperfing any tumultuous unlawful affemblies of perfons, threatening the peace of the realm and the fafety of the lives and properties of his Majefty's loyal fubjects wherefoever collected.

EXTRACT FROM AN ADDRESS TO THE PEOPLE OF IRELAND, PUBLISHED IN THE PRESS OF FEBRUARY 17, 1798.

" TRUST them not; remember what they promifed when Dungannon had alarmed them, *and how well they performed* the affurance they gave. The fame promifes they are again ready to make you, that they may throw the nation off its guard, and reduce you to your former fituation. It is not *your* fafety that they are confulting, but *their own.* Not three weeks fince, one of our mafters declared, that *reform* " was the watch-word of treafon;" with *the watch-word*

word of treafon then, *they* come forth, and effect to better *your* condition. Thus by their own rule, they become *traitors themfelves;* and of all traitors, thofe are the worft who would cajole thofe whom they cannot force, by duping them to their own defigns. While they thought you dif-united, and unable to refift tyranny, they reviled and in-fulted you; they provoked your patience, with every indig-nity and every violence; they dared you to oppofe their criminal career, and even *wifhed* to try their force with yours. Such it feems is their *love* of you! but at the name of *THE GREAT NATION,* they fink into their own worthlefsnefs: already they hear its thunders breaking on their heads, and fee its armies pouring deftruction on them. While thofe thunders rolled at a diftance, they defpifed the noife, for men are apt to be brave when they apprehend no danger; but as the found approaches, their dread encreafes with its nearnefs; and appalled at the power they had fo often defied, they lower the loftinefs of their air, and affume the tones of moderation.

" Well may they dread their enemies, for they know the extent of their enormous guilt, and the magnitude of their great offence! But their intended offer to conciliate proves two things; firft, their confcioufnefs of *your* ftrength, and *their own* imbecility; and fecondly, (although it is a fact they have long been in the habit of denying) that all power originates with the *people,* to whom at laft thofe that exer-cife it are compelled to refort."

[*It has been judged proper to reprint the following original* Profpectus *of the affociation of* United Irifhmen, *which was privately circulated by the firft founders of that Society in the month of* June 1791. *Whoever reads this with attention will require no farther proof that the deepeft and moft fyftematic Trea-fon, not only againft the Conftitution of this country, but againft the whole Order of Society in every country, was the grand ob-ject of that Fraternity from the firft moment of its being con-ceived.—It will be feen, that every aid which infernal ingenuity could furnifh for working on the paffions of the weak, the igno-rant, and the depraved, was deliberately adopted—that even in this embryo ftate the defign rifes to a height of revolutionary*
                                                                    boldnefs

boldnefs hardly equalled by the German Illuminati *themselves, and that all the horrible events which have since taken place in this country are nothing more than the practical development of this original project.*]

IDEM SENTIRE, DICERE, AGERE,

IT is proposed that at this conjuncture a SOCIETY shall be instituted in this city, having much of the secrecy, and somewhat of the ceremonial attached to Free Masonry—with so much secrecy as may communicate curiosity, uncertainty and expectation to the minds of surrounding men;—with so much impressive and affecting ceremony in all its internal œconomy, as, without impeding real business, may strike the soul through the senses, and addressing the *whole* man, may animate his philosophy by the energy of his passions.

Secrecy is expedient and necessary; it will make the bond of union more cohesive, and the spirit of this union more ardent and more condensed; it will envelope this dense flame with a cloud of gloomy ambiguity, that will not only facilitate its own agency, but will at the same time confound and terrify its enemies by their ignorance of the design, the extent, the direction, or the consequences. It will throw a veil over those individuals whose professional prudence might make them wish to lye concealed, until a manifestation of themselves became absolutely necessary. And, lastly, secrecy is necessary, because it is by no means certain that a country, so great a stranger to itself as Ireland, where the North and the South, and the East and West, meet to wonder at each other, is yet *prepared* for the adoption of one profession of Political Faith, while there may be individuals from each of these quarters ready to adopt such a profession, and to propagate it with their best abilities, when necessary—with their blood.

Our Provinces are perfectly ignorant of each other;—our Island is connected;—we ourselves are insulated; and the distinctions of rank, of property, and of religious persuasion, have hitherto been not merely lines of difference, but brazen walls of separation. We are separate nations met

met and fettled together, not mingled, but *convened*; an in-coherent mafs of diffimilar materials, uncemented, uncon-folidated, like the image which Nebuchadnezar faw with a head of fine gold, legs of iron, and feet of clay, parts that do not cleave to one another.

In the midft of an ifland, where Manhood has met and continues to meet with fuch fevere humiliation, where felfifh men, or claffes of men, have formed fuch malignant con-fpiracy againft Public Good, let one benevolent, beneficent confpiracy arife, one Plot of Patriots pledged by folemn abjuration to each other in the fervice of the People—the PEOPLE, in the largeft fenfe of that momentous word. Let the cement of this Conftitutional Compact be a principle of fuch ftrong attraction, as completely to overpower all acci-dental and temporary repulfions that take place between real Irifhmen, and thus to confolidate the fcattered and fhifting fand of Society into an adhefive and immoveable Caiffon, funk beneath the dark and troubled waters. It is by wan-dering from the few plain and fimple principles of Political Faith that our Politics, like our Religion, has become Preaching, not Practice, Words, not Works.

A Society, fuch as this, will difclaim thofe party appella-tions which feem to pale the human heart into petty com-partments, and parcel out into Sects and Sections, Common Senfe, Common Honefty, and Common Weal. As little will it affect any fpeculative, unimpaffioned, quiefcent be-nevolence. It will not call itfelf a Whig Club, or a Re-volution Society. It will not ground itfelf on a name in-dicative of a party, or an event well enough in the circum-ftances and in the feafon. It will not be an Ariftocracy af-fecting the language of Patriotifm, the rival of Defpotifm, for its own fake, not its irreconcileable enemy, for the fake of *us all*.

It will not, by views merely retrofpective, ftop the march of mankind, or force them back into the lanes and alleys of their anceftors. It will have an eye provident and profpec-tive, a reach and amplitude of conception commenfurate to the progreffive diffufion of knowledge, and at the fame time a promptitude in execution requifite in a life like this, fo fhort and fo fragile, in a nation like this, fo paffive and pro-craftinating. Let its name be the *IRISH BROTHERHOOD*. Let its general aim be to make the light of philanthropy, a pale and ineffectual light, *converge*, and by converging kin-dle into ardent, energetic, enthufiaftic love for Ireland; that

that genuine unadulterated enthufiafm which defcends from a luminous head to a burning heart, and impels the fpirit of man to exertions greatly good, or unequivocally great. For this Society is not to reft fatisfied in drawing fpeculative plans of reform and improvement, but to be practically bu- fied about the *means* of accomplifhment. Were the hand of Locke to hold from Heaven a fcheme of government moft perfectly adapted to the nature and capabilities of the Irifh Nation, it would drop to the ground a mere founding fcroll, were there no other means of giving it effect than its in- trinfic excellence. All true Irifhmen agree in *what* ought to be done, but how to get it done is the queftion.—This Society is likely to be a means the moft powerful for the promotion of a great end—what END ?

THE RIGHTS OF MEN IN IRELAND, the greateft hap- pinefs of the greateft number in *this ifland*, the inherent and indefeafible claims of every free nation, to reft in this nation—the *will* and the *power* to be happy—to purfue the Common-Weal as an individual purfues his private welfare, and to ftand in infulated independence, an imperatorial Peo- ple.——To gain a knowledge of the real ftate of this hete- rogeneous country, to form a fummary of the national will and pleafure in points moft interefting to national happinefs, and when fuch a fummary is formed, to put this *Doctrine* as fpeedily as may be into *Practice*, will be the purpofe of this Central Society, or Lodge, from which other Lodges in the different towns will radiate.

THE GREATEST HAPPINESS OF THE GREATEST NUM- BER—On the rock of this principle let this Society reft ; by this let it judge and determine every political queftion, and whatever is neceffary for this end, let it not be ac- counted hazardous, but rather our intereft, our duty, our glory, and our common religion. The Rights of Men are the rights of God, and to vindicate the one is to maintain the other. We muft be free in order to ferve Him whofe fervice is perfect freedom.

Let every Member wear, day and night, an Amulet round his neck, containing the great principle which unites the Brotherhood, in letters of gold, on a ribbon, ftriped with all the original colours, and inclofed in a fheath of white filk, to reprefent the pure union of the mingled rays, and the abolition of all fuperficial diftinctions, all co- lours and fhades of difference, for the fake of one illuftrious end. Let this Amulet of union, faith and honour depend
from

from the neck, and be bound about the body next to the ſkin and cloſe to the heart.

This is enthuſiaſm.—It is ſo; and who that has a ſpark of Hibernicifm in his nature, would not kindle into a flame of generous enthuſiaſm? Who, that has a drop of ſympathy in his heart, when he looks around him, and ſees how happineſs is heaped up in mounds, and how miſery is diffuſed and divided among the million, does not exclaim, Alas! for the ſuffering, and Oh! for the power to redreſs it? And who is there that has enthuſiaſm ſufficient to make an exclamation, would not combine with others as honeſt as himſelf, to make the will live in the act, and to ſwear— *WE WILL REDRESS IT*—Who is there? Who?-

The firſt buſineſs of the Brotherhood will be to form a tranſcript, or digeſt, of the doctrine which they mean to ſubſcribe, to uphold, to propagate, and reduce to practice. It is time for Ireland to look her fortune in the face, not with turbulent oſtentation, but with fixed reſolution to live and die Freemen.—Let then thoſe queſtions be agitated and anſwered fully and fairly which have been wilfully concealed from us by intereſted perſons and parties, and which appear terrible only by being kept in the dark. Always armed with this principle, that it is the duty of the people to eſtabliſh their rights, this Society will carry it along with them in their courſe, as the Sybil did the branch of gold, to avert or to diſperſe, every vain fear, or every unreal terror.

What are the *means* of procuring ſuch a Reform in the Conſtitution as may ſecure to the People their rights moſt effectually and moſt ſpeedily?

What is the plan of Reform moſt ſuited to this country?

Can the renovation in the Conſtitution, which we all deem neceſſary, be accompliſhed by the *ways* of the Conſtitution? " The evil," ſays Junius, " lies too deep to be " cured by any remedy, leſs than ſome great convulſion " which may bring back the Conſtitution to its original " principles, or utterly deſtroy it." Is this opinion ſtill truer when applied to *this* country? or is it falſe?

Who are the People?

Can the right of changing the Conſtitution reſt any where but in the original conſtitutive power—the People?

Can the will of the People be known but by full and fair convention, to be conſtituted on the plan which will come recommended on the moſt popular authority?

Z

What

What are the rights of Roman Catholics, and what are the immediate duties of Proteſtants reſpecting theſe rights? Are the Roman Catholics generally or partially *capaces Libertatis?* and if not, What are the ſpeedieſt means of making them ſo?

Is the Independence of Ireland nominal or real, a barren right, or a fact regulative of national conduct and influencing national character?

Has it had any other effect than raiſing the value of a houſe, and making it more ſelf-ſufficient, at the expence of the People?

Is there any middle ſtate between the extremes of union with Britain and total ſeparation, in which the rights of the People can be fully eſtabliſhed and reſt in ſecurity?

What is the form of Government that will ſecure to us our rights with the leaſt expence and the greateſt benefit?

By the BROTHERHOOD are theſe queſtions, and ſuch as theſe, to be determined. On this determination are they to form the chart of their Conſtitution, which with honour and good faith they are to ſubſcribe, and which is to regulate their courſe.——Let the Society at large meet four times in the year, and an acting Committee once a month, to which all Members ſhall be invited. Let theſe meetings be *convivial*, but not the tranſitory patriotiſm of deep potation; *confidential*, the heart open and the door locked; *converſational*, not a debating ſociety. There is too much haranguing in this country already: a very great redundance of ſound. Would that we ſpoke a little more laconically, and acted a little more emphatically; and we ſhall do ſo, when our aim is at ſomething nobler and fairer than even the ſublime and beautiful of Mr. Burke:—the ſublimity of Common-ſenſe—the beauty of Common-weal.

Our Society ſhould at firſt be very chaſte and cautious in the ſelection of Members, ſhunning equally the giddineſs of the boy, and that ſullen indifference about the public good which comes on with decline of years, looking around for thoſe who are competent, and with reſpect to themſelves content, yet zealous and perſevering; not venal, not voracious, not confined in their manners and their morality to the pale of a profeſſion, not idle philanthropiſts, who fidget round the globe with their favourite adage; not thoſe who are bound down by obedience to that wizard word *Empire*, to the ſovereignty of two ſounding ſyllables; but honeſt, honourable

honourable *Irifhmen*, of whatever rank, of whatever religion, who know Liberty, who love it, who wifh to have it,
and who will have it.—Members fhould be admitted only by
an unanimous ballot, and perhaps once a year there fhould
be a general re-election.

The *external* bufinefs of this Society will be, 1ft. Publication, in order to propagate their principles and effectuate
their ends. All papers for this purpofe to be fanctioned
by the Committee, and publifhed with no other defignation
of character than—ONE OF THE BROTHERHOOD.—2dly,
Communication with the different towns to be affiduoufly
kept up, and every exertion ufed to accomplifh a *National
Convention* of the People of Ireland, who may profit by paft
errors, and by many unexpected circumftances which have
happened fince the laft meeting.—3dly, Communication
with fimilar Societies abroad, as the Jacobin Club in Paris,
the Revolution Society in England, the Committee for Reform in Scotland. Let the nations go abreaft. Let the in-
terchange of fentiment among mankind concerning the
rights of man be as immediate as poffible. A correfpondence with diftinguifhed men in Britain, or on the Conti-
nent, will be neceffary to enlighten us, and ought to be
cherifhed. Eulogies on fuch men as have deferved well of
their country *until death*, fhould be from time to time delivered by one of the Brotherhood, their works fhould live in
a library to be formed by this Society, and dedicated to Liberty, and the Portraits of fuch men fhould adorn it. Let
the fhades of the mighty dead look down and confecrate
our Meetings. The Athenians were accuftomed to faften
their edicts to the ftatues of their anceftors. Let our
Laws and Liberties have a fimilar attachment, taking heed
always to remember what has been always too much forgotten—that *We* are to be anceftors ourfelves; and as our bodies moulder down after fepulture, merely to pafs into new
forms of life, let our fpirits preferve a principle of anima-
tion to pofterity, and germinate from the very grave.

What is the time moft applicable for the eftablifhment of
this Inftitution? Even NOW. " Le grand art eft dans
" l'apropos." Why is Adminiftration fo imperious? Becaufe the Nation does not act. The Whig Club is not a
transfufion from the People. We do not thoroughly *under-
fland* that Club, and they do not *feel* for us. When the Ariftocracy come forward, the People fall backward; when the
People come forward, the Ariftocracy, fearful of being
left

left behind, ihfinuate themfelves into our ranks, and rife
into timid leaders, or treacherous auxiliaries. They mean
to make us their inftruments. ·Let us rather make them *our*
inftruments. One of the two muft happen. The People
muft ferve the purpofes of Party, or the Party muft emerge
in the mightinefs of the People, and Hercules will then
lean upon his club.

On the 14th of July, the day which fhall ever comme-
morate the French Revolution, let this Society pour out
their firft libation to European Liberty, eventually the Liberty of the World, and with their hands joined in each
other, and their eyes raifed to Heaven, in his prefence who
breathed into them an ever-living foul, let them fwear to
maintain the rights and prerogatives of their nature as men,
and the right and prerogative of Ireland as an Independent
People.—" Dieu et *mon* Droit !" is the motto of Kings,—
" Dieu et la Liberté !" exclaimed Voltaire, when he firft
beheld Franklin his Fellow-Citizen of the World.—" Dieu
et *nos* Droits !"—Let Irifhmen cry aloud to each other——
The cry of Mercy—of Juftice—and of Victory.

June, 1791.